# LIFE SKILLS FOR TEENS

MASTERING SOCIAL SKILLS, RELATIONSHIPS, TECHNOLOGY, FINANCIAL LITERACY, HEALTHCARE, INDEPENDENT LIVING, AND MUCH MORE!

AC BRADFORD

© Copyright 2024 - All rights reserved.

The content contained within this book may not be reproduced, duplicated or transmitted without direct written permission from the author or the publisher.

Under no circumstances will any blame or legal responsibility be held against the publisher, or author, for any damages, reparation, or monetary loss due to the information contained within this book, either directly or indirectly.

**Legal Notice:**

This book is copyright-protected. It is only for personal use. You cannot amend, distribute, sell, use, quote, or paraphrase any part or the content within this book, without the consent of the author or publisher.

**Disclaimer Notice:**

Please note the information contained within this document is for educational and entertainment purposes only. All effort has been executed to present accurate, up-to-date, reliable, complete information. No warranties of any kind are declared or implied. Readers acknowledge that the author is not engaged in the rendering of legal, financial, medical, or professional advice. The content within this book has been derived from various sources. Please consult a licensed professional before attempting any techniques outlined in this book.

By reading this document, the reader agrees that under no circumstances is the author responsible for any losses, direct or indirect, that are incurred as a result of the use of the information contained within this document, including, but not limited to, errors, omissions, or inaccuracies.

# CONTENTS

*Introduction*     5

1. FINANCIAL LITERACY FOR TEENS     9
   1.1 Creating a Budget on an Allowance or Part-Time Salary     10
   1.2 Understanding Bank Accounts and Debit Cards     11
   1.3 Basics of Credit and Credit Scores     14
   1.4 Recognizing Financial Scams and Fraud     16
   1.5 Saving for Short and Long-Term Goals     18

2. BUILDING AND MAINTAINING RELATIONSHIPS     21
   2.1 Identifying Healthy vs. Toxic Friendships     21
   2.2 Communication Strategies for Conflict Resolution     24
   2.3 Setting Boundaries with Friends and Peers     25
   2.4 Understanding Romantic Relationships     28
   2.5 Building Trust and Empathy in Relationships     29

3. EMOTIONAL INTELLIGENCE AND SELF-DEVELOPMENT     33
   3.1 Developing Empathy and Emotional Awareness     36
   3.2 Coping with Failure and Building Resilience     38
   3.3 Cultivating a Growth Mindset     39
   3.4 Setting and Achieving Personal Development Goals     42

4. MASTERING SOCIAL SKILLS     45
   4.1 Active Listening Techniques     47
   4.2 Making Sincere Apologies     49
   4.3 Asking for Help with Confidence     51
   4.4 Handling Social Anxiety in Public Settings     53

5. HEALTH AND PERSONAL WELL-BEING     55
   5.1 Navigating Doctor's Appointments with Ease     58
   5.2 Stress Management Techniques for Teens     60
   5.3 Recognizing and Addressing Mental Health Issues     62

6. NAVIGATING TECHNOLOGY AND DIGITAL
   SPACES                                                    67
   6.1 Managing Screen Time for Better Balance               70
   6.2 Protecting Personal Information Online                72
   6.3 Identifying and Responding to Cyberbullying           74
   6.4 Using Technology for Educational Success              76

7. EDUCATIONAL AND CAREER PLANNING                           79
   7.1 Effective Study Habits and Time Management            82
   7.2 Exploring Higher Education Options                    84
   7.3 Writing a Professional Resume and Cover Letter        86
   7.4 Preparing for Job Interviews with Confidence          88
   7.5 Exploring Different Career Paths                      89

8. INDEPENDENT LIVING SKILLS                                 93
   8.1 Essential Home Maintenance Skills                     94
   8.2 Understanding Nutrition and Meal Planning             96
   8.3 Basic Cooking Techniques for Beginners                98
   8.4 Organizing and Decluttering Your Space               100
   8.5 Understanding Rent Agreements and Housing
       Options                                              102
   8.6 Managing Utility Bills and Subscriptions             104

9. COMMUNITY ENGAGEMENT AND SOCIAL
   RESPONSIBILITY                                           107
   9.1 The Importance of Volunteering and
       Community Service                                    108
   9.2 Understanding Social Causes and Advocacy             110
   9.3 Practicing Environmental Sustainability              113
   9.4 Engaging in Civic Duties and Responsibilities        114

10. PLANNING FOR THE FUTURE                                 117
    10.1 Navigating the Transition from School to Work      118
    10.2 Financial Planning for Future Stability            120
    10.3 Long-Term Goal Setting and Life Planning           123

    *Conclusion*                                            127
    *References*                                            131

# INTRODUCTION

A few years ago, I met a teen named Alex at a local community event. Alex was bright and full of potential, yet overwhelmed by the thought of growing up. Over several weeks, he confided in me about his anxieties: managing money, navigating friendships, and even cooking a simple meal seemed daunting. It was a familiar story that I had heard from many teens and young adults who felt unprepared for the real world. Alex's story stayed with me, inspiring me to write this book.

The purpose of this book is simple yet vital: to serve as a guide for teens transitioning into adulthood. Life skills are the foundation of personal growth, independence, and confidence. They empower you to face challenges head-on and thrive in any situation. This book is your toolkit for building those skills.

Who is this book for? It's for teens like Alex, standing on the brink of adulthood and seeking guidance. It's for young adults who want to sharpen their skills and gain confidence. Parents and educators will also find value here, as it offers insights and strategies to support the young people in their lives. Each group will find practical advice tailored to their needs.

Today's teens face a unique set of challenges. Did you know a recent study found that nearly 60% of teens feel unprepared to manage their finances? Or many struggle with the impact of technology on their social lives? These challenges are real, and they can feel overwhelming. But with the right tools, you can navigate them successfully.

This book is a guide to overcoming fears and anxiety. Imagine starting with feelings of uncertainty and ending with a strong sense of capability. You'll learn how to manage your money, communicate effectively, and live independently. Along the way, you'll build confidence and discover your potential. By the end, you'll feel equipped to tackle whatever life throws your way.

What does this journey look like? It begins with understanding financial literacy. You'll learn the basics of budgeting, saving, and investing. Next, we'll dive into social skills. You'll find tips for building meaningful relationships and communicating clearly. Then, we'll cover technology, healthcare, and independent living. Each chapter builds on the last, offering a complete toolkit for success.

I am passionate about helping teens and young adults like you. My commitment is to provide practical, easy-to-follow guidance. I believe in the power of these skills to change lives, and this book is the culmination of that belief. I'm excited to share it with you.

As you turn the pages, I encourage you to approach this journey with an open mind and a willingness to learn. Embrace the challenges and celebrate your progress. This is your chance to grow into the confident, capable adult you're meant to be.

The key takeaway is clear: mastering life skills is critical to achieving independence and success. It's about building a life you're proud of and stepping into adulthood with confidence. Let's start this journey together.

# 1

# FINANCIAL LITERACY FOR TEENS

*"Do not save what is left after spending, but spend what is left after saving."*

— WARREN BUFFETT

A high school junior, Gabby landed her first part-time job at a local café. It was exciting—her first taste of earning her own money. But soon, she found herself puzzled by where all her paychecks went. By the end of each month, she was left scratching her head, wondering why her bank balance was always so low. Gabby's story is all too familiar. Earning money is one thing, but managing it is an entirely different skill set. Gabby, with a part-time job, and also teens who rely on an allowance, can begin to develop a sense of what it means to be responsible for their finances. This chapter guides you on taking control of your finances, ensuring that each dollar you earn works for you, not the other way around.

Financial literacy is a cornerstone of independence. It's about understanding how to manage money effectively to afford what you need today and save for tomorrow. For teens stepping into the world of financial responsibility, this skill is crucial. Whether saving up for a new phone, planning a trip, or even considering college expenses, knowing how to handle money wisely will set you up for success. So, let's dive into the essentials of creating a budget on a part-time salary.

## 1.1 CREATING A BUDGET ON AN ALLOWANCE OR PART-TIME SALARY

Understanding where your money goes begins with categorizing your income and expenses. Start by tracking the money you earn from your part-time job or allowance. This is your income, the foundation of your budget. Next, categorize your expenses into fixed and variable. Fixed expenses don't change monthly, like your phone bill or subscriptions. Variable expenses fluctuate—think snacks, outings, or new clothes. Knowing the difference helps you see where you might be overspending. Once you categorize your expenses, subtract them from your income to determine your disposable income. After covering your essentials, this is what you have left, and it's key for planning savings or extra spending.

Now that you know where your money is going, it's time to set realistic financial goals. Think about what you want to achieve in the short and long term. Maybe you're saving for a concert ticket next month or planning for college expenses. Set specific goals and assign a portion of your disposable income to each. This way, you can see progress and stay motivated. Remember, goals should be achievable. Start small and build up. The satisfaction of reaching one goal fuels the drive to tackle another.

To keep track of your budget and goals, use tools that make the process easier. Spreadsheets are a great way to start. They allow you to manually track your spending, giving you a clear picture of your financial habits. Consider budgeting apps like Mint or YNAB if you prefer something more automated. These apps categorize spending, alert you when you're nearing limits, and offer insights into spending trends. Some apps like GoHenry or Gimi provide educational content, helping you better understand financial responsibility. Choose a method that fits your style and stick with it. Consistency is key.

Life is unpredictable. Budgets should be flexible, allowing you to adjust when unexpected expenses arise. Suppose you must buy a last-minute gift or pay for an unplanned event. Knowing how to reallocate funds without derailing your financial goals is essential. Look at areas where you might cut back temporarily, like dining out or entertainment. This doesn't mean sacrificing all your fun; it means making informed choices to stay on track. Flexibility in budgeting ensures you're prepared for surprises without compromising your long-term plans.

## 1.2 UNDERSTANDING BANK ACCOUNTS AND DEBIT CARDS

Stepping into the world of bank accounts can feel like learning a new language. Yet, understanding this language is crucial for managing your finances effectively. At the core of financial management are checking and savings accounts. A checking account is your go-to for everyday transactions. It's like a digital wallet, allowing you to deposit your paycheck, pay bills, and easily purchase. Many banks offer student checking accounts with perks like no monthly fees or minimum balance requirements. This makes them a perfect starting point for teens and young adults who are just beginning to manage their finances independently. On the other hand, a savings account is where you stash money for future goals. Thanks to the interest it earns, it's designed to help your money grow over time. Consider opening a high-yield savings account, which offers a higher interest rate than a regular savings account, maximizing the growth of your savings.

With the rise of technology, online banking has become a fundamental tool. It provides the convenience of managing your accounts anytime, anywhere. Online banking lets you view account balances, transfer money, and even deposit checks using your smartphone. Setting up automatic bill payments can save you time and ensure you never miss a due date, which is especially handy if you're juggling school, work, and other commitments. Regularly monitoring your account activity is another essential habit. This helps you keep track of your spending and alerts you to any unauthorized transactions, adding an extra layer of security to your finances. Embracing these features can simplify your financial life and give you more control over your money.

When it comes to everyday purchases, debit cards are your best friend. They draw directly from your checking account, making them a convenient alternative to carrying cash. Unlike credit cards, debit cards don't involve borrowing money, so you won't incur debt or interest charges. This makes them an excellent tool for managing spending within your means. Use a debit card for groceries, gas, or catching a movie with friends. Think of it as your key to accessing the funds in your checking account but with the added benefit of tracking your transactions digitally, which helps you stick to your budget.

However, using a debit card requires careful management to avoid overdraft fees, which occur when you spend more than your account balance. Such fees can quickly add up, creating unnecessary financial strain. One effective strategy is to maintain a buffer balance in your account. This means keeping a small amount of money set aside that you don't touch, acting as a financial cushion. Another tip is to regularly check your account balance before making a purchase, ensuring you have sufficient funds. Some banks offer overdraft protection, linking your checking account to a savings account to cover any shortfall, although this may involve fees. Staying informed about your account balance and understanding the terms of your bank's services can prevent costly surprises.

**Interactive Element: Bank Account Checklist**

To help you get started, here's a checklist to ensure you're making the most of your bank account features:

- Open a student checking account to avoid unnecessary fees.
- Consider a high-yield savings account to grow your money.
- Set up online banking for easy access and management.
- Enable automatic bill payments for convenience and reliability.
- Check your account balance regularly to stay on top of your finances.
- Use a debit card for everyday purchases to manage spending.
- Keep a buffer balance to avoid overdraft fees.

Familiarizing yourself with bank accounts and debit cards might initially seem complex, but with practice and regular monitoring, they become invaluable allies in managing your finances effectively.

## 1.3 BASICS OF CREDIT AND CREDIT SCORES

Credit scores, while seemingly complex, are essential in the realm of finance. This numerical figure, which ranges from 300 to 850, tells the story of your financial reliability. It plays a significant role in your ability to secure loans and lease residences, and can even influence employment opportunities. Grasping the mechanics behind credit scores is crucial to achieving financial independence. A myriad of factors influence your credit score: your payment history, the total debt you carry, the duration of your credit history, the diversity of your credit accounts, and the frequency of new credit applications. Each element contributes to a comprehensive profile of your financial responsibility. Regular, timely payments, for instance, enhance your creditworthiness, according to lenders. In contrast, habitual late payments or utilizing a high percentage of your available credit can depict you as a high-risk borrower. It's imperative to monitor your credit score consistently. Services such as Credit Karma or annualcreditreport.com offer complimentary access to your credit reports, allowing you to stay abreast of your financial status and make informed decisions. Embarking on the journey of building credit at a young age is pivotal for financial independence. A practical approach is to obtain a secured credit card. This type of card is backed by a cash deposit you make upfront, which usually sets your credit limit. This security deposit significantly lowers the risk for the issuer while enabling you to cultivate a credit history. By using this card for minor, manageable expenses and paying the balance each month, you exhibit fiscal prudence, gradually enhancing your credit score. Opting for a secured credit card as your introduction to credit management establishes a solid groundwork for future financial ventures.

Understanding the distinction between credit and debit cards is also key to managing your credit effectively. Unlike debit cards, which withdraw money directly from your checking account, credit cards function as short-term loans for every transaction. Your management of a credit card, including how much of your limit you use and your payment consistency, is reported to credit bureaus. Careful use of credit cards, such as using less than 30% of your credit limit and paying off balances in full, can have a positive impact on your credit history, demonstrating to lenders that you are adept at managing borrowed funds. However, it's crucial to exercise caution, as the flexibility of credit spending can easily lead to debt accumulation if not monitored closely. In essence, mastering the fundamentals of credit and diligently managing your credit cards can significantly influence your financial literacy and independence. Adopting responsible credit habits early on sets the stage for a future filled with broader financial possibilities and stability.

Managing credit card debt requires discipline and foresight. One of the most effective strategies is to pay the full balance each month before the due date. This practice not only prevents high-interest charges but also keeps your credit utilization low, both of which are beneficial for your credit score. Additionally, limiting the number of credit cards you own is wise, as having too many can make tracking spending more complicated. If you find yourself struggling with debt, consider consolidating it with a balance transfer card offering a lower interest rate. By staying organized and proactive, you can maintain healthy credit and avoid the pitfalls of excessive debt.

Understanding and managing credit is a fundamental aspect of financial literacy. It empowers you to build a positive credit history, opening doors to various financial opportunities in the future. With careful planning and responsible habits, navigating the world of credit becomes less intimidating and more empowering.

## 1.4 RECOGNIZING FINANCIAL SCAMS AND FRAUD

In today's digital world, the threat of financial scams looms large, especially for teens and young adults. Many find themselves vulnerable to cunning fraudsters due to a lack of experience or awareness. Imagine receiving an email that appears to be from your bank. It requests that you verify your account details to prevent it from being frozen. This is a classic phishing scam, where the goal is to steal your sensitive information. Fraudsters craft emails that look legitimate, using logos and language that mimic official communications. The unsuspecting victim, worried about their account, might hurriedly click the link and enter their details, unknowingly handing over the keys to their finances. Many banks will tell you that they will never request any kind of verification by email. If you receive a request for verification by email, always check the sender's email address. Most times, you will find a long, complicated email address that has nothing to do with the bank. Lottery scams are another prevalent trap. They lure you with promises of massive winnings but require a fee upfront to claim the prize. It's a cruel trick that exploits the excitement of unexpected fortune only to leave you empty-handed and out of pocket.

Safeguarding personal information is crucial in today's interconnected landscape. You can start by shredding documents containing sensitive information before you discard them. This simple act can prevent dumpster divers from retrieving your data. In the digital realm, using secure passwords is imperative. A strong password combines uppercase and lowercase letters, numbers, and symbols, creating a complex barrier that deters unauthorized access. Regularly updating passwords adds an extra layer of protection. Also, you can enable two-factor authentication whenever possible. This feature requires a second form of verification, such as a code sent to your phone, before granting access to your accounts. Taking these steps significantly reduces the risk of falling victim to cyber theft.

Acting quickly and decisively is important if you suspect you've been targeted by a scam or fraud attempt. You can start by reporting the incident to the authorities and your financial institutions. Many banks have dedicated fraud departments that can freeze your account to prevent unauthorized transactions. Similarly, the Federal Trade Commission (FTC) provides resources and guidance on how to handle scams and identity theft. Reporting protects you and helps prevent the scam from spreading to others. Document your interactions with the scammer and provide this information when reporting. These details can aid investigations and lead to the fraudsters' apprehension.

Staying informed is another powerful defense against scams. The landscape of fraud is ever-evolving, with new tactics appearing regularly. Continuously educating yourself about the latest scams can keep you one step ahead. Follow reputable financial news sources that report on emerging fraud trends and offer advice on how to stay safe. Organizations like the Better Business Bureau and the Consumer Financial Protection Bureau publish warnings and updates on common scams. Subscribing to their alerts can provide valuable insights and tips. Additionally, discussing fraud awareness with friends and family can expand your collective knowledge, creating a more informed community that can support each other.

In this digital age, awareness and vigilance are your best allies in the fight against financial fraud. You can safeguard your financial well-being by recognizing common scams, protecting your personal information, and responding swiftly to threats. Please stay proactive and informed to make sure that you navigate the financial world securely and confidently.

## 1.5 SAVING FOR SHORT AND LONG-TERM GOALS

Picture this: You've just received your paycheck, and the temptation to spend it all on the latest tech gadget or a night out with friends is strong. But what if you could enjoy today while also securing your financial future? This is where a well-crafted savings plan comes into play. Establishing a savings plan that aligns with your goals is the backbone of financial security. Begin by setting up automatic transfers from your checking account to your savings account. This simple step ensures that you consistently save a portion of your earnings without having to think about it. Consider saving a percentage of each paycheck, perhaps starting with 10%. Over time, as your income grows, you can increase this percentage, steadily building your savings.

Understanding how interest works in savings accounts can make a significant difference. Interest is the reward for saving money, calculated as a percentage of your balance. Over time, this can grow your savings without any extra effort on your part. Compounding interest, which means you earn interest on both your initial deposit and the interest it has already earned, can significantly boost your savings over the long term. Choose a savings account that offers competitive interest rates to maximize this benefit. Even a small difference in rates can lead to substantial growth over the years. Consider consulting your bank or using online comparison tools to find the best options available.

An emergency fund is the financial safety net everyone should have. It's not about saving for a rainy day; it's about being ready for unexpected life challenges—like a medical emergency or urgent car repair—that can happen anytime. Start small, perhaps setting aside a few hundred dollars as your initial goal. Once you've achieved this, aim to gradually build a fund covering three to six months' living expenses. This might seem daunting, but breaking it down into smaller, manageable amounts makes it achievable. Regular contributions, even small ones, add up over time, providing peace of mind knowing you have a buffer against the unexpected.

Balancing saving and spending is an art form that, when mastered, provides both security and satisfaction. It starts with a clear understanding of your needs versus wants. Needs are essentials like food, shelter, and transportation. Wants are those non-essential items that enhance your life but aren't necessary for survival. Prioritize your spending by ensuring your needs are met first, then allocate what's left to your savings and discretionary spending. This approach allows you to enjoy the present while also preparing for the future. It may require some sacrifice and discipline, but the rewards—financial stability and the freedom to seize opportunities as they arise—are well worth the effort.

As you navigate the intricacies of saving, remember that these practices are not just about financial prudence but about empowering yourself with choices and opportunities in the future. By setting up automatic savings, understanding the power of interest, building an emergency fund, and striking a balance between saving and spending, you lay a strong foundation for long-term success. Once established, these habits become second nature, guiding you toward a future filled with possibility and peace of mind.

# 2

# BUILDING AND MAINTAINING RELATIONSHIPS

*"The quality of your life is the quality of your relationships."*

— TONY ROBBINS

## 2.1 IDENTIFYING HEALTHY VS. TOXIC FRIENDSHIPS

When I was in high school, I had a friend named Jamie. We met during freshman year and quickly became inseparable. Jamie had a knack for making everyone laugh, and I admired her charisma. But as time went on, I noticed a pattern. Every time I shared an achievement, she would downplay it or shift the focus back to herself. At first, I shrugged it off, thinking maybe I was just being sensitive. But these moments began to weigh on me, and I realized Jamie wasn't the supportive friend I thought she was. This experience taught me a lot about the nature of friendships and the importance of recognizing healthy and toxic traits.

Understanding the characteristics of a healthy friendship is crucial. A supportive friendship thrives on mutual respect and support. In such relationships, there's a balance where both individuals respect each other's boundaries, opinions, and feelings. Encouragement plays a vital role; a good friend celebrates your successes and picks you up during setbacks. It's about being present in each other's lives, offering a shoulder to lean on, and sharing in the joy of achievements. Trustworthiness and empathy are cornerstones of healthy friendships. These traits allow friends to be vulnerable and honest, fostering a deeper connection. Humor and congeniality also enhance friendships, creating an atmosphere of joy and understanding.

On the flip side, toxic friendships can be harmful to your well-being. They often manifest through constant criticism and belittling, where one friend undermines the other's confidence. Manipulative behavior is another red flag. It involves guilt-tripping and shifting blame, leaving you feeling responsible for things beyond your control. Such friends might also isolate you from others, making you dependent on their approval. These toxic traits erode self-esteem and create an imbalance in the relationship. Recognizing these warning signs early is essential to protect yourself emotionally and mentally. Understanding these patterns helps you maintain healthy relationships and distance yourself from those that harm you.

Self-reflection plays a pivotal role in evaluating friendships. It's an opportunity to assess your contributions and the dynamics within the relationship. Journaling is a powerful tool for this. After spending time with friends, jot down your feelings and thoughts. Reflect on whether these interactions leave you feeling uplifted or drained. This practice helps identify patterns and clarifies whether the friendship is nurturing or toxic. It also encourages personal growth by highlighting areas that you might want to work on to improve as a friend. By understanding your role, you can foster healthier connections and set boundaries that protect your well-being.

If you can't gradually let a toxic relationship end by spending less time together, you may feel you should end it with a conversation. It's never an easy thing to do, but if you feel It's necessary to maintain your personal dignity and mental health, and you're sure you want to do it, you can start by preparing an outline of a script for the conversation. This helps you think through your feelings clearly and makes sure you cover all the points you feel are important. Be honest yet respectful, focusing on how the friendship makes you feel rather than blaming the other person. Express gratitude for the good times shared, but emphasize the need for change. It's crucial to stay calm, even if the other person's response is defensive or hostile. As hard as this may be, it will help you feel better about yourself once you've closed this chapter if you choose to do it this way. Remember, it's okay to protect your well-being and seek relationships that bring out the best in you.

**Reflection Section**

Consider the friendships in your life. Are there any that consistently leave you feeling drained or undervalued? Take a moment to reflect on the interactions you have with those friends. Use the prompts below to guide your thoughts:

- How do you feel after spending time with this friend?
- Can you identify patterns of criticism or manipulation?
- Do you often feel the need to justify your actions or opinions?
- Is there mutual respect and support in the relationship?

Write down your thoughts and consider whether these friendships are nurturing or harmful. You can use this as a guide for future relationships.

## 2.2 COMMUNICATION STRATEGIES FOR CONFLICT RESOLUTION

Conflict is inevitable in any relationship, but how we handle it can make all the difference. The key lies in active communication, a skill that enables you to express feelings openly and listen to others with empathy. One powerful tool in this regard is using "I" statements. Instead of saying, "You never listen to me," try saying, "I feel ignored when my thoughts aren't acknowledged." This subtle shift in language focuses on your feelings rather than placing blame, reducing defensiveness and opening the door to honest dialogue. It encourages a more productive conversation where both parties feel heard and respected.

Finding common ground during a conflict can transform a standoff into a collaboration. It begins with recognizing shared goals and interests. Maybe you and your friend both want to enjoy time together without misunderstandings. Acknowledging this shared desire can shift the focus from the problem to a solution. Brainstorming together fosters a sense of unity. Sit down and list potential solutions, no matter how unconventional they may seem. This collective problem-solving eases tensions and strengthens the bond as you work towards a mutually beneficial outcome. It's about turning "me versus you" into "us against the problem."

Compromise is the cornerstone of conflict resolution, balancing differing needs and desires. It involves identifying non-negotiables —those things you can't compromise on—and distinguishing them from flexible points where you can bend. Perhaps you need your study time undisturbed, but you can be flexible about meeting up later for a movie. This clarity helps you communicate your priorities and understand the other person's. Compromise doesn't mean giving up what matters; it's about finding a middle ground where both sides feel valued and respected. Once cultivated, it's a skill that can enhance not just friendships but all kinds of relationships.

De-escalating tense situations requires a calm approach, especially when emotions run high. A timeout can be a valuable tool here. It's not about avoiding the issue but taking a moment to cool off and gather your thoughts. Stepping back allows you to process emotions and approach the situation with a clearer mind. During this break, engage in relaxing activities—take a walk, practice deep breathing, or listen to calming music. By the time you return to the conversation, you're better equipped to discuss the issue rationally and constructively. It's about providing space for emotions to settle, leading to more productive discussions.

When handled with care and communication, conflicts can strengthen relationships rather than weaken them. Developing these strategies helps resolve disputes and fosters growth and understanding. Communication is more than just talking; it's about connecting on a deeper level, ensuring that the relationship remains strong and resilient even when disagreements arise.

## 2.3 SETTING BOUNDARIES WITH FRIENDS AND PEERS

Understanding personal boundaries is a cornerstone of healthy relationships. Boundaries are the invisible lines that define where you end and another person begins. They protect your personal space, emotions, and energy, ensuring that interactions remain respectful and balanced. Emotional boundaries, for instance, safeguard your feelings and thoughts, ensuring others don't take advantage of your emotional generosity or impose their issues on you. Physical boundaries, meanwhile, involve your personal space and comfort with physical touch. Recognizing these boundaries helps maintain a sense of self while interacting with others. Without clear boundaries, friendships can become overwhelming, leading to feelings of resentment or exploitation.

It's helpful if you can express your boundaries effectively. You can start by practicing assertive communication, which involves being honest and straightforward about your needs without being aggressive. This means calmly stating your limits and expectations. Role-playing scenarios with peers can be a helpful exercise to practice this skill. For instance, if a friend often borrows your belongings without asking, you might say, "I feel uncomfortable when my things are taken without my permission. Please ask next time." This direct but respectful approach clarifies your boundaries and sets the tone for future interactions. Practicing these conversations in a safe setting can build confidence, making it easier to express your needs in real situations.

Respecting others' boundaries is equally important. It reflects your understanding and acknowledgment of their personal space and emotional needs. Before you share someone's personal information, ask for permission. For example, if you want to share a friend's story or photo online, check with them first. This simple act of asking respects their privacy and shows that you value their comfort and consent. Such practices foster trust and mutual respect, reinforcing the foundation of a healthy friendship. It's a reciprocal process—by respecting others, you encourage them to respect your boundaries in return, creating a balanced and respectful dynamic.

When boundaries are crossed, addressing the issue is necessary to restore balance and trust in the friendship. Begin by having a follow-up conversation to reaffirm your boundaries. Choose a calm moment when both parties are relaxed. Express how the boundary violation affected you and restate your needs. For instance, "When you shared my personal story without asking, I felt hurt. I need to know my privacy is respected." This approach is not about confrontation but clarification and resolution. It's about ensuring that both parties understand and respect each other's limits. By addressing issues promptly and constructively, you prevent misunderstandings from festering and maintain the integrity of the relationship.

*Interactive Element: Boundary Setting Exercise*

Try this exercise to help define and communicate your personal boundaries effectively:

- **Reflect on Your Boundaries:** Spend a few minutes thinking about situations you felt uncomfortable or taken advantage of. What boundary was crossed?
- **Write Down Your Boundaries:** List these boundaries, focusing on emotional, physical, and social aspects.
- **Role-Play Conversations:** With a trusted friend, practice assertively expressing these boundaries. Use phrases like "I need" or "I feel uncomfortable when."
- **Seek Feedback:** Ask for feedback on your communication style and clarity after role-playing.

This exercise helps solidify your understanding of personal boundaries, making it easier to express and maintain them in real-life situations. By practicing these skills, you equip yourself with the tools to navigate friendships respectfully and confidently.

## 2.4 UNDERSTANDING ROMANTIC RELATIONSHIPS

Navigating the complex world of romantic relationships can feel both exhilarating and daunting. At the heart of any healthy romantic relationship lies mutual respect and equality. These elements ensure that both partners feel valued and heard, setting a solid foundation for a relationship that can withstand challenges. Respect manifests in everyday interactions—by honoring each other's thoughts, feelings, and boundaries, you create a space of safety and trust. Equality, on the other hand, involves sharing power and decision-making. It means that no one person dominates the relationship, and both partners contribute to its growth and direction. When respect and equality are present, a relationship flourishes, allowing both individuals to thrive.

Developing emotional intimacy is a journey of understanding and closeness. It involves peeling back layers to reveal vulnerabilities while maintaining your individuality. Discussing personal boundaries early on is crucial in this process. It sets the tone for interacting and understanding each other's needs. Sharing your stories, fears, and dreams builds a connection bridge, but it's important to keep your sense of self intact. Being open about your boundaries ensures that your partner knows what makes you comfortable and what doesn't, fostering a deeper connection without losing your identity. This balance allows you to grow together while respecting the space you each need.

Recognizing unhealthy patterns in a romantic relationship is vital to maintaining emotional health. Jealousy and possessiveness often masquerade as affection but can quickly turn toxic. These feelings stem from insecurity and lead to controlling behavior, which undermines trust and respect. Frequent arguments and controlling behavior are red flags that should not be ignored. They signal a power imbalance where one partner might try to manipulate or dominate the other. It's crucial to be aware of these signs and address them head-on. Open conversations about concerns and feelings can sometimes resolve misunderstandings, but consistently unhealthy dynamics may require reevaluating the relationship's viability.

While difficult, a romantic relationship can be ended with maturity and respect. It starts with honest communication about your feelings and the reasons for the breakup. Choose a time and place where you both can speak openly without distractions. Be direct but compassionate, focusing on your feelings rather than blaming others. Maintaining personal well-being post-breakup is essential. Surround yourself with supportive friends and family, engage in activities that bring you joy, and allow yourself time to heal. It's okay to grieve the end of a relationship, but remember that this is also an opportunity for growth and self-discovery. By approaching breakups with respect and care, you preserve your dignity and set the stage for healthier relationships in the future.

## 2.5 BUILDING TRUST AND EMPATHY IN RELATIONSHIPS

Trust is the backbone of any meaningful relationship, yet it doesn't appear overnight. It's the result of consistent actions and reliability. You might remember a time when a friend promised to help you with a project or be there when you needed them. When they followed through, it strengthened your bond and reassured you of their dependability. Building trust is about these small yet significant promises kept over time. It's showing up when you say you will, being honest even when it's difficult, and being a constant support. Each promise fulfilled is like a brick laid in the foundation of your relationship, slowly building a structure that can withstand challenges and time.

Practicing empathy is another pillar of strong relationships. It's about seeing the world through another person's eyes, feeling their emotions, and understanding their perspectives. When a friend shares their troubles, listening to understand rather than just to reply makes all the difference. It means putting aside your own judgments and focusing entirely on their words and feelings. This active listening creates a safe space where they feel valued and heard. Empathy isn't just about agreement; it's about connection and compassion. It's a skill that deepens friendships and fosters an environment of mutual respect and support, transforming how we interact with those around us.

Trust, once broken, is challenging to rebuild but not impossible. It requires open and honest communication about feelings and intentions. Begin by acknowledging the hurt caused and the role you played in it. Sincerely apologize and express your commitment to change. Rebuilding trust is not just about words but actions that demonstrate reliability and sincerity over time. It involves patience and consistency; the other person needs time to see that you are genuinely committed to restoring the relationship. This process can be painful but ultimately rewarding as it clears the path for a stronger and more resilient bond built on a foundation of transparency and genuine effort.

Empathy also plays a powerful role in resolving conflicts. When tensions run high, it's easy to get caught up in defending your own viewpoint. But stepping into the other person's shoes can shift the dynamic entirely. Reflective listening can be incredibly effective, where you repeat what you've heard to confirm understanding. It validates emotions and shows the other person that their feelings matter to you. This approach diffuses tension and encourages a deeper understanding of each other's perspectives. By focusing on empathy, conflicts become opportunities for growth and learning, rather than divisive battles, fostering stronger, more harmonious relationships.

As we close this chapter on building and maintaining relationships, remember that trust and empathy are the keys to nurturing connections that last. These elements transform interactions into meaningful exchanges and lay the groundwork for deeper bonds. As we move forward, these lessons will serve as a foundation for tackling other aspects of life.

# 3

# EMOTIONAL INTELLIGENCE AND SELF-DEVELOPMENT

*"Self-awareness doesn't stop you from making mistakes—it allows you to learn from them."*

— UNKNOWN

Imagine standing in front of your class, palms sweating, as you prepare to present your project. Your heart races, and doubt creeps in. What if they don't like it? What if I stumble over my words? For many of us, these moments of vulnerability can feel overwhelming, but they also present an opportunity to build both self-esteem and self-confidence. Understanding these concepts is vital to personal growth.

Self-esteem is how we value and perceive ourselves, while self-confidence is the belief in one's ability to perform specific tasks. Balancing the two can open doors to new experiences, help you handle setbacks with grace and foster independence.

Self-esteem is foundational. It's your overall sense of personal value and self-worth. When you feel good about who you are, it naturally influences how you interact with the world. High self-esteem is linked to resilience, emotional well-being, and a positive self-image. It's about accepting yourself, flaws and all, and recognizing that you're deserving of love and respect. Conversely, self-confidence is more situational, reflecting how you feel about your abilities in specific areas. You might feel confident in math class but less so on the basketball court. Understanding this distinction helps you identify where you can grow and where you already excel.

Boosting self-confidence involves practical, daily exercises. Positive affirmations are a powerful tool. Start your day by looking in the mirror and saying, "I am capable," or "I am worthy of success." These affirmations, though simple, reinforce a positive self-image and can gradually reshape how you perceive your abilities. Practicing small acts of bravery is also effective. Speaking up in class or joining a new club can be terrifying, but these experiences build confidence over time. Each small victory chips away at self-doubt, proving to yourself that you can face challenges head-on.

Negative self-perceptions can be persistent, but they are not invincible. Keeping a journal to track self-critical thoughts is a helpful exercise. Write down negative thoughts as they arise, then challenge them with evidence. If you think, "I'm terrible at this," ask yourself, "What proof do I have?" Often, you'll find these thoughts lack a solid foundation. Reframing negative thoughts into constructive ones is another vital strategy. Instead of thinking, "I failed," consider, "I learned what didn't work and can try a new approach." This shift in perspective encourages growth and fosters resilience, turning setbacks into stepping stones.

Recognizing and celebrating personal achievements is crucial in building self-esteem. Create a "success jar" where you jot down achievements, big or small, on slips of paper. Did you ace a test or help a friend in need? Write it down and add it to the jar. Over time, this collection serves as a tangible reminder of your progress and accomplishments. Reflecting on these successes boosts your self-esteem, reminding you of your capabilities and the positive impact you have on the world. It's a visual testament to your growth, reinforcing the message that you are capable and worthy.

*Reflection Section: Self-Esteem and Confidence Journal*

Try this reflection exercise to deepen your understanding of self-esteem and self-confidence:

- **Daily Affirmations:** Write down three positive affirmations to recite each morning.
- **Acts of Bravery:** List three brave actions you can take this week.
- **Challenging Negative Thoughts:** Identify one negative thought and reframe it positively.
- **Success Jar Contribution:** Write down one recent achievement and place it in your success jar.

Use these reflections to track your growth and celebrate your journey toward enhanced self-esteem and self-confidence. This practice boosts your personal development and strengthens your emotional well-being, setting the stage for continued success.

## 3.1 DEVELOPING EMPATHY AND EMOTIONAL AWARENESS

Imagine sitting with a friend who's sharing a personal story. They're upset, and you feel a tug inside urging you to understand and support them. This is empathy, a powerful tool for connecting with others. Empathy is about tuning into someone else's feelings and experiences. It helps you see the world through their eyes, fostering deeper connections and understanding. It's not just about feeling what others feel but also about understanding why they feel that way. Empathy is crucial for building strong relationships and navigating social situations with sensitivity. There are two main types of empathy: cognitive and emotional. Cognitive empathy involves understanding another person's perspective, while emotional empathy involves sharing emotions. Balancing both allows you to relate to others while maintaining your emotional balance.

Enhancing your emotional awareness can be transformative. It starts with recognizing and understanding your emotions, which can be achieved through mindfulness meditation. This practice involves focusing on the present moment and observing your thoughts and feelings without judgment. Find a quiet space, close your eyes, and take deep breaths. Notice how your emotions rise and fall like waves in the ocean. This awareness helps you manage emotions rather than being overwhelmed by them. Emotion wheel exercises also aid in identifying and naming feelings. An emotion wheel is a visual tool that organizes emotions into categories, helping you pinpoint what you're really experiencing. By naming your emotions, you gain power over them, making it easier to address and regulate them effectively.

Listening with empathy transforms conversations. Reflective listening is one such technique, where you repeat back what someone has said to ensure understanding. For example, if a friend says, "I'm frustrated with my grades," you might respond, "It sounds like you're upset about your performance in school." This shows that you're paying attention and validates their feelings. It creates a safe space for open dialogue and encourages deeper sharing. Practicing empathic listening involves putting aside your judgments and focusing entirely on the speaker. It's about being present and offering support without trying to fix the problem. This approach strengthens bonds and fosters trust, as people feel genuinely heard and understood.

Recognizing emotional triggers is key to managing reactions. Emotional triggers are events or situations that provoke a strong emotional response, often stemming from past experiences. Identifying these triggers helps you anticipate and prepare for emotional reactions. Start by paying attention to physical cues, such as a racing heart or clenched fists, which signal an emotional response. Reflect on situations consistently leading to intense emotions and explore the underlying reasons. Understanding these patterns allows you to respond, choosing actions that align with your values rather than react. Techniques like deep breathing or pausing can help you regain control and approach the situation with clarity.

Empathy and emotional awareness are intertwined, enhancing your ability to connect with others and understand yourself. By practicing these skills, you cultivate a greater sense of compassion and emotional intelligence, enriching your interactions and personal growth.

## 3.2 COPING WITH FAILURE AND BUILDING RESILIENCE

Imagine failing a test you studied hard for. The sinking feeling of disappointment can be overwhelming, but what if failure wasn't the end? What if it was simply a stepping stone? This mindset shift is crucial. Redefining failure as a learning opportunity means viewing setbacks as a natural part of growth. Analyze what went wrong and identify areas for improvement. Maybe it was a lack of preparation or misinterpreting the material. You can develop strategies to overcome these factors next time by pinpointing them. This process prepares you for future challenges and enhances problem-solving skills.

Building resilience involves developing the mental fortitude to bounce back from adversity. Flexibility and adaptive thinking are vital components. Imagine a tree bending in the wind rather than breaking. Similarly, resilience allows you to adapt to change and recover from setbacks. Practice seeing obstacles as opportunities to grow. Cultivate adaptive thinking by challenging yourself with new experiences and learning from each one. Additionally, creating a support network provides encouragement during tough times. Surround yourself with friends, family, and mentors who uplift you. Their perspectives and support can offer guidance and reassurance when you face challenges.

Adopting a "fail-forward" mentality means embracing failure as a step toward success. Instead of fearing mistakes, view them as chances to learn and improve. Start by setting small, incremental goals that build confidence. Achieving these goals reinforces the belief that progress is possible, even when faced with setbacks. This approach encourages a proactive attitude, where each failure becomes a lesson rather than a roadblock. By taking deliberate steps forward, you cultivate resilience and perseverance, essential traits for navigating life's uncertainties.

Learning from role models who have overcome failure can be incredibly inspiring. Take J.K. Rowling, for example. Before Harry Potter became a global phenomenon, Rowling faced numerous rejections from publishers. Her manuscript was turned down twelve times before finding success. Yet, she persisted, using each rejection as motivation to improve her writing. Today, her story is a testament to the power of resilience and determination. Similarly, Steve Jobs faced setbacks, such as being ousted from Apple, the company he co-founded. Instead of giving up, he used the experience to fuel innovation and eventually returned, leading Apple to unprecedented success. These stories remind us that failure is not the end but rather a part of the process toward achieving greatness. By studying the journeys of those who have succeeded despite setbacks, you can draw inspiration and learn valuable lessons.

In embracing these strategies, remember that resilience is not about avoiding failure but learning to thrive despite it. It involves reframing setbacks as opportunities for growth, creating supportive networks, and adopting a forward-thinking mindset. Each step you take in this direction strengthens your ability to navigate challenges and emerge stronger on the other side.

## 3.3 CULTIVATING A GROWTH MINDSET

Imagine you're handed a puzzle—a daunting array of pieces that, at first glance, seems impossible to piece together. But instead of giving up, you decide to view it as a challenge. This is the essence of a growth mindset. Unlike a fixed mindset, which sees abilities as static and unchangeable, a growth mindset thrives on the belief that skills and intelligence can be developed through dedication and hard work. It's the difference between saying, "I'm just not good at math," and, "I can improve if I practice." This mindset opens doors to personal and professional success by embracing challenges as opportunities to grow rather than obstacles to avoid. Those with a growth mindset see effort as a path to mastery, not an indication of inadequacy. They understand that setbacks are not failures but steps on the path to improvement.

Shifting from a fixed mindset to a growth mindset involves practical strategies. Start by welcoming challenges. When faced with a difficult task, rather than shrinking away, ask yourself, "What can I learn from this?" This shift in perspective transforms obstacles into learning experiences. Embrace the discomfort, knowing that it's a sign of growth. Another effective approach is to view effort as a necessary component of learning. Effort isn't just about working hard; it's about persisting through difficulties and seeking creative solutions. Celebrate the process rather than just the outcome. Each attempt, successful or not, brings you closer to your goals. By focusing on improvement rather than perfection, you cultivate resilience and adaptability.

Encouraging curiosity and lifelong learning is central to nurturing a growth mindset. Curiosity fuels exploration and discovery. It pushes you to ask questions and seek answers, expanding your horizons. Try exploring new hobbies or subjects of interest. If you've always been interested in photography, pick up a camera and capture the world around you. Engaging in activities outside your comfort zone enhances your skills and builds confidence. It's about the thrill of discovering something new, the joy of learning for its own sake. This approach fosters a love for learning that extends beyond the classroom, enriching your life in countless ways.

Self-reflection is a powerful tool for recognizing personal growth and areas for improvement. Keeping a growth journal helps track your progress and reflect on your experiences. Regularly jot down your thoughts, challenges, and breakthroughs. Celebrate your successes, no matter how small, and analyze areas that need work. This habit encourages a mindset of continuous improvement, reinforcing the belief that growth is possible and ongoing. By documenting your journey, you gain insight into your development, recognizing patterns and identifying strategies that work best for you. This reflective practice enhances self-awareness and motivates you to keep pushing forward.

***Interactive Element: Growth Mindset Reflection***

Take a moment to reflect on your mindset and growth:

- Think about a recent challenge you faced. How did you approach it?
- Identify a skill you'd like to develop. What steps can you take to improve?
- Write about a time when effort led to success. How did it feel?
- Consider an area where you can push your boundaries. What's one new activity you can try this week?

You can use these prompts to guide your reflections and encourage a growth-oriented approach to everyday situations. By consistently practicing these strategies, you reinforce the principles of a growth mindset, paving the way for lifelong learning and development.

## 3.4 SETTING AND ACHIEVING PERSONAL DEVELOPMENT GOALS

Stepping into self-improvement begins with understanding where you stand. Identifying areas for personal development requires introspection and honesty. Using self-assessment tools to pinpoint your strengths and weaknesses is helpful. These tools can range from simple quizzes highlighting your personality traits to more detailed assessments evaluating skills like communication or leadership. Focus on areas you wish to enhance as you engage with these tools. You may want to become more organized, improve your public speaking, or learn a new language. Recognizing these areas is the first step in crafting a plan for personal growth. This self-awareness highlights where you have room to grow and reinforces what you're already excelling at, setting a balanced foundation for development.

Once you've identified your focus areas, the next step is creating an action plan. This plan serves as your roadmap, guiding you toward your goals. Start by breaking down each goal into smaller, actionable steps. If your aim is to improve time management, begin by setting specific tasks like creating a daily schedule or using a planner. Each step should feel manageable and clear, providing a sense of direction amidst the chaos of everyday life. Setting deadlines and milestones keeps your progress on track. These aren't rigid dates meant to pressure you but rather checkpoints to celebrate your forward momentum. As you achieve each milestone, you're not just marking time but witnessing your growth, reinforcing the belief that change is indeed possible.

However, as you pursue personal development, obstacles will inevitably arise. Common barriers include procrastination and a lack of motivation. These hurdles can stall progress and breed frustration. To combat procrastination, try breaking tasks into smaller chunks and tackling them one at a time. This makes the workload more manageable and more approachable. A lack of motivation often stems from losing sight of why you started. Reconnect with your initial inspiration—whether it's a personal vision or a role model. Visual reminders, like a dream or vision board, can reignite your drive. Additionally, establishing a routine can anchor your efforts, turning small actions into habits that propel you forward, even on days when motivation wanes.

Recognizing and celebrating milestones along the way is crucial. Each achievement, no matter how small, deserves acknowledgment. It's easy to focus on what's left to do and overlook what's been accomplished. Yet, celebrating these victories reinforces your dedication and hard work. Consider rewarding yourself when you reach a significant milestone. This could be as simple as taking a day off to relax or treating yourself to something special. These rewards aren't just indulgences; they affirm your progress and commitment. They serve as tangible reminders of your capabilities, boosting your confidence and encouraging you to continue pursuing your goals with vigor.

As this chapter closes, reflect on the importance of setting and achieving personal development goals. These goals act as beacons, guiding you through the complexities of growth and self-improvement. They remind you that progress is a continuous process. Whether small or large, each step you take contributes to the bigger picture of who you aspire to become. As we look ahead, our focus will shift, exploring new personal and professional growth dimensions.

# 4

# MASTERING SOCIAL SKILLS

*"The most important single ingredient in the formula of success is knowing how to get along with people."*

— THEODORE ROOSEVELT

Picture this: you walk into a room full of strangers, each engaged in their conversations. The air buzzes with chatter, and you feel a sudden flutter of nerves. How do you introduce yourself? How do you make a good impression? Social introductions are often daunting but are the gateway to building connections. Whether it's a new school, your first job, or a community event, the ability to introduce yourself confidently can set the tone for future interactions. First impressions matter. They play a crucial role in opportunities, influencing how others perceive you academically and professionally. They're not just about the words you say; your posture, handshake, and eye contact all contribute to the impression you leave behind.

A proper handshake can be the first step toward forming a positive impression. It's about balance—not too firm, yet not too weak. A handshake conveys confidence and respect, signaling you are present and engaged. Make direct eye contact as you introduce yourself. Eye contact shows interest and sincerity, creating an instant connection. It's a silent yet powerful message that you're open and attentive. Introduce yourself with confidence. State your name clearly and warmly. Confidence doesn't mean being loud or boastful; it's about being assured in your presence and words. How you carry yourself during these moments can leave a lasting impact, setting the stage for meaningful interactions.

Crafting a personal introduction that is both concise and engaging can make all the difference. Think of it as your verbal business card. Start with a simple formula: name, interest, and a fun fact. For instance, "Hi, I'm Alex. I'm passionate about photography, and I once captured a photo of a rare bird in my backyard." This structure introduces who you are and gives a glimpse into your personality, sparking conversation. Sharing a fun fact can be a conversation starter, inviting others to learn more about you. It's about sharing enough to pique curiosity while allowing dialogue to unfold naturally.

Understanding social cues is vital in navigating introductions. People communicate as much through body language and facial expressions as they do through words. Recognize open body language—uncrossed arms, relaxed posture, and nodding indicate receptiveness and engagement. Conversely, crossed arms and averted eyes can signal discomfort or disinterest. By observing these cues, you can gauge the comfort level of others and adjust your approach accordingly. A warm smile and relaxed demeanor can invite others to feel at ease. Social interactions are dynamic, and being attuned to these non-verbal signals helps you navigate them with empathy and awareness.

Group introductions add another layer of complexity. Entering a group conversation requires tact and timing. Wait for a natural pause in the discussion before introducing yourself. A simple, "Hi everyone, I'm Jamie, it's great to meet you all" can suffice. It's important to read the room and find an organic moment rather than interrupting the flow. When it's time to exit, do so politely. Thank the group for their time, and express your interest in continuing the conversation later. This approach respects the group dynamic and leaves a positive impression, even as you step away.

***Interactive Element: Social Introduction Exercise***

Try this exercise to master your social introductions:

- **Create Your Introduction:** Write down your name, one interest, and a fun fact about yourself.
- **Practice in Front of a Mirror:** Observe your body language and adjust it to convey confidence.
- **Role-Play with a Friend:** Simulate different introduction scenarios, such as a casual meet-up or a formal event.
- **Reflect on Feedback:** Ask your friend for your introduction and body language feedback.

Use this exercise to refine social skills and enhance confidence in various settings. By practicing these elements, you prepare yourself for engaging and meaningful interactions.

## 4.1 ACTIVE LISTENING TECHNIQUES

Listening actively can transform the interaction into something deeply meaningful when you engage in a conversation. Active listening is more than just hearing words; it's about fully immersing yourself in the moment, understanding the speaker, and responding thoughtfully. This practice is vital for building strong relationships and understanding others more deeply. It involves giving your full attention to the speaker, nodding occasionally to show you're following along, and using verbal affirmations like "I see" or "Go on" to encourage them. These gestures show that you value what they're saying, fostering an environment of trust and connection. Asking clarifying questions is another aspect of active listening. If something isn't clear, gently inquire, "Could you explain that further?" This demonstrates your interest and ensures you grasp the conversation's nuances.

However, effective listening doesn't come without its challenges. Distractions are everywhere, from buzzing phones to wandering thoughts. These barriers can disrupt your focus and prevent you from truly understanding the speaker. Minimizing distractions is crucial. When someone is talking, put your phone away, and direct your attention solely to them. Create a mental space where only the conversation exists, free from external interruptions. This presence allows you to catch subtle cues and respond appropriately, making the speaker feel valued and heard. Overcoming these barriers requires conscious effort and practice, but the rewards are profound, leading to stronger and more meaningful connections.

Paraphrasing and reflecting are key techniques in demonstrating understanding. When someone shares their thoughts, rephrase their message in your words and reflect it back. This might sound like, "What I hear you saying is that you're feeling overwhelmed with your workload." This approach confirms that you're on the same page and allows the speaker to correct misunderstandings. It reinforces the idea that you're genuinely engaged and invested in their perspective. Paraphrasing also will enable you to digest and process the information, deepening your comprehension and empathy. By articulating their thoughts back to them, you affirm their feelings and encourage further sharing, solidifying your role as a supportive listener.

Listening with empathy elevates the conversation to a new level. It involves placing yourself in the speaker's shoes, feeling their emotions, and understanding their viewpoint. This empathetic approach goes beyond mere words; it's about experiencing the world through their eyes. When a friend talks about a tough day, imagine how it must feel for them. Acknowledge their emotions and validate their experiences. This doesn't mean you must agree, but it shows that you care about their feelings. Empathy fosters a deeper connection, creating a safe space for open dialogue. Practicing empathy in listening strengthens relationships and enhances your emotional intelligence, making you more attuned to others' needs and perspectives.

Active listening is a powerful tool that transforms conversations into meaningful exchanges. By practicing these techniques, you can build stronger, more empathetic connections with those around you. As you continue to develop your listening skills, you'll find that understanding and supporting others becomes second nature.

## 4.2 MAKING SINCERE APOLOGIES

Apologies are powerful tools in repairing relationships and fostering understanding. Genuine apologies require sincerity and thoughtfulness, involving several vital components. First, acknowledging the mistake is crucial. This means clearly stating what you did wrong without making excuses. It's about owning up to your actions and the impact they had. For instance, instead of saying, "I'm sorry if I upset you," say, "I'm sorry for what I said, and I realize it was hurtful." This clarity shows that you understand the specific issue and are taking responsibility. Expressing genuine remorse means showing that you truly feel sorry for the harm caused. This involves empathy and understanding how your actions affect the other person. Offering to make amends is the final step. It demonstrates a commitment to righting the wrong, whether it's through a direct act or a promise to change your behavior. By including these elements, your apology becomes more than just words; it becomes a meaningful step toward rebuilding trust and connection.

Common pitfalls can undermine an apology, rendering it insincere or ineffective. One frequent mistake is using "if" statements that imply blame or doubt, such as, "I'm sorry if you felt offended." This phrasing suggests that the issue lies with the other person's feelings rather than your actions. Instead, use language that takes full responsibility for your behavior. Additionally, avoid shifting blame or making assumptions about the other person's experience. A sincere apology focuses on your actions and their consequences, not defending your intentions or minimizing the impact. By avoiding these pitfalls, you ensure that your apology communicates genuine regret and a willingness to make things right.

The medium through which you deliver an apology can significantly affect its reception. Face-to-face apologies are generally more effective for serious matters or when the relationship is close. They allow immediate interaction, where body language and tone convey sincerity and empathy. However, a phone call or video chat can suffice when distance or timing makes an in-person apology impractical. Digital apologies, such as emails or text messages, might be more appropriate for minor misunderstandings or when a quick response is needed. However, they lack the emotional nuance that comes with vocal expression. Choose the medium based on the nature of the mistake and the relationship involved. I think the key is to make sure that your apology feels personal and thoughtful, regardless of the format.

Rebuilding trust after a mistake involves more than just a heartfelt apology. It requires consistent actions that demonstrate your commitment to change. Trust is fragile and must be nurtured through behavior that aligns with your words. This means actively avoiding repeating mistakes and consciously trying to strengthen the relationship. Show through your actions that you have learned from the experience and are dedicated to making amends. Patience is essential, as rebuilding trust takes time. It involves being reliable and showing up for the other person, reinforcing the idea that they can count on you moving forward. These efforts help mend the rift caused by the mistake, gradually restoring the trust that was lost.

## 4.3 ASKING FOR HELP WITH CONFIDENCE

Recognizing when to ask for help is an important skill that can often feel daunting. It involves understanding your personal limits and knowing when a task or situation has exceeded your current capabilities. This recognition is not an admission of failure but a step toward growth and learning. For instance, when you find yourself spending hours on a math problem with no progress, that's a cue. It's a sign that seeking assistance could provide the clarity needed to move forward. Identifying such moments requires self-awareness and honesty about your strengths and areas where you could benefit from someone else's expertise. Acknowledging these limits is not about giving up; it's about leveraging your resources to achieve your goals more effectively.

It's a good idea when you ask for help to be thorough and considerate. When reaching out, it's important to be clear about what you need and respect the other person's time and ability to assist. Framing your request positively can make a significant difference. Start with a phrase like, "I would appreciate it if you could help me understand this concept," which communicates your needs clearly while expressing gratitude in advance. This approach opens the door to a collaborative interaction, setting a tone of mutual respect. Articulating your request in a way that acknowledges their expertise and willingness to help can make the process smoother and increase the likelihood of receiving a positive response. It's about crafting a considerate and concise request, ensuring that your needs are understood without imposing on the other person.

The fear of rejection is a common barrier when asking for help. It often stems from the worry that others might view you as incapable or burdensome. Overcoming this anxiety involves reframing the way you perceive rejection. Instead of seeing it as a personal failure, view it as an opportunity to learn and grow. Practice self-affirmations to build confidence. Remind yourself that seeking help is a strength, not a weakness, and that everyone sometimes needs assistance. Phrases like "I am learning and growing" or "I am capable of overcoming challenges" can reinforce a positive mindset. By acknowledging your courage and resilience, you empower yourself to reach out without fear, knowing that rejection is simply a part of the learning process, not a reflection of your worth.

Expressing gratitude after receiving help is crucial in maintaining and strengthening relationships. It shows appreciation for the support offered and reinforces the bond between you and the other person. A simple thank-you can go a long way, but taking an extra step can make it even more meaningful. Sending a follow-up thank-you note, whether handwritten or digital, adds a personal touch that acknowledges their contribution to your growth. In your note, mention specifically how their assistance helped you, making the gratitude genuine and specific. This expression solidifies the relationship and encourages continued support and collaboration. It's a small gesture that fosters goodwill and reinforces the value of helping others, creating a positive cycle of support and gratitude.

## 4.4 HANDLING SOCIAL ANXIETY IN PUBLIC SETTINGS

For many, entering a crowded room feels like stepping onto a stage without a script. The sheer volume of people, chatter, and movement can trigger social anxiety. This feeling isn't just about being shy; it's a more intense experience where the mind races with worries about being judged or making a mistake. Recognizing what sets off these feelings is a crucial step. Crowded environments, unfamiliar faces, or being the center of attention often top the list of triggers. Knowing this can help you prepare and manage your reactions. By identifying these triggers, you can start to anticipate situations that might cause discomfort, allowing you to develop strategies to cope before anxiety takes hold.

When anxiety creeps in, having a toolbox of coping strategies can make all the difference. Deep breathing is a powerful tool. It seems simple, but it works wonders in calming the body's fight-or-flight response. Try this: inhale deeply through your nose for four counts, hold for four, and exhale slowly through your mouth for another four. This practice helps steady your breath and heart rate, bringing a sense of calm. Another technique is grounding, which involves focusing on your surroundings to anchor yourself in the present. Look around and silently name several things you can see, touch, and hear. This sensory focus pulls your mind away from the anxiety and back to the now, reducing overwhelming feelings.

Facing anxiety-provoking situations gradually is an effective way to build resilience. Start with smaller gatherings where the stakes feel lower. Maybe it's a small group of friends or a familiar setting like a local café. As you grow more comfortable, slowly increase the size and unfamiliarity of the settings you enter. This step-by-step approach allows you to build confidence over time. Each successful interaction, no matter how small, is a victory that strengthens your ability to handle more challenging situations. It's about taking small steps forward and expanding your comfort zone without overwhelming yourself. By pacing yourself, you gain control and learn to manage anxiety at your own speed.

Relying on support systems is vital when navigating social anxiety. Friends and family can offer encouragement and reassurance, providing a safety net when you feel anxious. Creating a "safe person" plan can be particularly effective. You can choose someone you trust to accompany you to social events. Knowing they're there can ease your mind, allowing you to participate more freely. This person can offer a listening ear, provide a comforting presence, or even help you exit a situation if it becomes too overwhelming. Their support acts as a buffer against anxiety, reminding you that you're not alone. Building a support network helps cultivate confidence and courage in facing social challenges.

As this chapter closes, remember that social skills are like muscles—they strengthen with use and care. Whether handling anxiety, listening actively, or making sincere apologies, each skill forms a part of how we connect with others. As we move forward, we'll explore new ways to navigate the world and its challenges, continuing to build the foundation of skills that empower and uplift us.

# 5

# HEALTH AND PERSONAL WELL-BEING

*"Health is not just about what you're eating. It's also about what you're thinking and saying."*

— UNKNOWN

Imagine it's a bright morning, and you're getting ready for the day. You look in the mirror, splash some water on your face, and suddenly realize you have a big presentation at school. You feel a twinge of anxiety, but you smile at your reflection, remembering the confidence a good personal hygiene routine gives you. Personal hygiene is more than just cleanliness; it's about cultivating a sense of self-assurance and well-being. It's a routine that protects you from illness and helps you embrace the world with poise.

A solid hygiene routine is crucial for your physical health and self-esteem. Daily cleansing prevents skin issues and combats the increased body odor that may accompany puberty. During this time, hormonal changes such as those driven by estrogen in females and testosterone in males can intensify body odor and can trigger acne. Regular hygiene practices like bathing and using deodorant help mitigate these effects, ensuring you feel fresh and confident. Clean clothes and fresh breath do more than just improve your appearance; they boost your self-image and can significantly affect how others perceive you. Feeling good about your outward presentation fosters a positive mindset, contributing to your overall self-worth.

Establishing a consistent hygiene routine begins with a structured daily schedule. Consider starting your morning with a shower or bath and a skincare routine tailored to your needs. Begin by washing your face with a gentle cleanser to remove overnight oils and impurities. Follow with a moisturizer that includes SPF to protect your skin from harmful sun rays throughout the day. In the evening, cleanse your skin again to remove dirt and makeup, and apply a nourishing night cream to support skin repair while you sleep. Regular hair care is equally important. Depending on your hair type, you can set up a routine that involves washing, conditioning, and occasionally deep conditioning to maintain hair health and manageability. Grooming practices such as brushing your teeth twice daily and flossing support oral health and prevent cavities, while regular nail trimming keeps your hands clean and tidy.

When it comes to choosing hygiene products, it's essential to select those that suit your individual needs. Understanding the ingredients in skincare products can help you make informed decisions. For example, if you have sensitive skin, look for hypoallergenic or fragrance-free products. Those with dry skin might benefit from moisturizers containing hyaluronic acid, which helps retain moisture. When picking a deodorant, consider your skin type. If you have sensitive skin, opt for formulas free of alcohol or aluminum, which can cause irritation. Deodorants with sweat-control properties might be more effective for those leading active lifestyles. Reading labels and understanding what works best for your body ensures you use products that enhance your hygiene routine without causing adverse effects.

Adjusting your hygiene routine based on daily activities can help you stay fresh and confident, no matter what the day brings. After engaging in sports or physical activities, a quick freshening up can make a significant difference. Keep travel-sized hygiene products handy, such as facial wipes or dry shampoo, to manage sweat and oil when you're on the go. These products provide a temporary solution until you can complete your routine. If you anticipate a long day, consider carrying a small deodorant and mouthwash in your bag for a quick refresh. Adapting your routine to fit your lifestyle ensures you can maintain your hygiene standards and confidently face each day.

*Interactive Element: Personal Hygiene Checklist*

Creating a personalized hygiene checklist can support your routine:

- **Morning Routine:** Shower, cleanse the face, apply moisturizer with SPF, brush the teeth, and use deodorant.
- **Evening Routine:** Remove makeup, cleanse face, apply night cream, floss, brush teeth.
- **Weekly Tasks:** Wash hair, trim nails, exfoliate skin (as needed).
- **On-the-Go Essentials:** Travel-sized deodorant, facial wipes, dry shampoo, mouthwash.

This checklist can help you establish and maintain a hygiene routine tailored to your needs. By incorporating these practices into your daily life, you ensure you're always prepared to present your best self, no matter the challenges or opportunities.

## 5.1 NAVIGATING DOCTOR'S APPOINTMENTS WITH EASE

Imagine you're preparing for a doctor's appointment. Whether you're dealing with a lingering cold or just going for a routine check-up, preparation can transform an intimidating experience into a manageable task. You can start by making a list of symptoms and questions. This might sound simple, but it's surprisingly effective. Write down every symptom, no matter how minor it seems. Did you notice a persistent cough? Or maybe a weird rash? These details help your doctor understand your condition better. If there are specific questions about your health or treatment, jot them down, too. This ensures you won't forget to ask during the appointment, making the most of your time with the healthcare provider.

Bringing necessary medical records and insurance information is another essential step. Gather any recent test results, medication lists, and previous diagnoses. These documents offer your doctor a comprehensive view of your health history. This information becomes even more crucial if you're visiting a new doctor. Don't forget your insurance card, as it's needed for billing and coverage verification. Organize everything in a folder or digital file for easy access. Being prepared with all the necessary paperwork streamlines the appointment and demonstrates responsibility and readiness, leaving a positive impression on your healthcare provider.

Communicating effectively with healthcare providers is key to receiving the best care. It starts with how you describe your symptoms. Practice articulating your condition clearly and accurately. Use specific language. Instead of saying, "I feel sick," try, "I have a sharp pain in my lower back that worsens when I sit." This detail helps the doctor make an informed diagnosis. If the doctor uses medical jargon that confuses you, don't hesitate to ask for clarification. It's okay to say, "Could you explain that in simpler terms?" Doctors appreciate when patients actively participate in their care, and clear communication ensures you understand the treatment plan.

Understanding medical recommendations involves more than just listening. It's about interpreting and following through on the advice given. Start by carefully reading prescription labels. They contain important information about dosage, timing, and potential side effects. Misunderstanding these instructions can lead to ineffective treatment or unwanted complications. Follow post-appointment instructions to the letter. If your doctor recommends rest, medication, or a follow-up, adhere to these guidelines. Adhering to medical advice ensures the best possible outcomes, promoting faster recovery and supporting overall health.

Managing appointment-related anxiety is a common challenge. Many people feel uneasy about visiting the doctor, but several strategies can ease this tension. Breathing exercises are a simple yet effective tool. Before your appointment, find a quiet space. Inhale deeply through your nose, hold it for a moment, and exhale slowly through your mouth. Repeat this process several times until you feel calmer. This exercise helps reduce nervousness, allowing you to approach the appointment with a clear mind. Visualization can also help. Picture yourself in the waiting room, calm and composed. Imagine the appointment going smoothly. This mental preparation can alleviate stress, making the experience less daunting.

Doctor's appointments don't have to be a source of dread. With the right preparation and mindset, they can become an opportunity to take charge of your health.

## 5.2 STRESS MANAGEMENT TECHNIQUES FOR TEENS

Imagine a day filled with back-to-back classes, a pile of homework, and the expectation to excel in extracurricular activities. Add to that the pressure to maintain friendships and social status, and it's no wonder stress can feel overwhelming. Recognizing these sources of stress is the first step in managing them effectively. School-related pressures are a primary cause, with deadlines and exams creating a constant sense of urgency. The workload can sometimes feel insurmountable, leading to anxiety about meeting expectations. Beyond academics, social expectations, and peer pressure can also weigh heavily. The desire to fit in and be accepted by peers adds another layer of stress, often leaving teens feeling torn between who they are and who they think they should be. Identifying these stressors is crucial because it allows you to tackle them head-on rather than letting them silently build up.

Once you've pinpointed what's causing stress, developing coping mechanisms can help alleviate the burden. Journaling is a powerful tool for stress relief, offering a private space to express thoughts and emotions. Writing about your day and feelings or creating lists of things you're grateful for can provide clarity and perspective. This practice helps release pent-up emotions and identify patterns in your thoughts and behaviors that contribute to stress. Mindfulness and meditation exercises are also beneficial. These practices encourage you to focus on the present moment, reducing the noise of anxious thoughts. A simple exercise involves closing your eyes, taking deep breaths, and concentrating on the sensation of the air filling and leaving your lungs. Even just a few minutes daily can make a significant difference, calming the mind and offering a fresh perspective on stressful situations.

Incorporating physical activity into your routine can also be a game-changer in managing stress. Exercise releases endorphins, the body's natural mood lifters, which can help reduce feelings of stress and anxiety. Engaging in daily walks or runs boosts your mood and provides a break from daily pressures. It's a time to clear your head, enjoy some fresh air, and perhaps even discover new parts of your neighborhood. If running isn't your thing, consider other activities like dancing, yoga, or cycling. The key is to find something you enjoy, making it easier to incorporate into your routine. Regular physical activity enhances your physical health and strengthens your mental resilience, preparing you to face challenges with a clearer mind.

Building a support network is another essential aspect of stress management. Having friends or family members you can turn to when feeling overwhelmed is invaluable. These individuals provide a listening ear, offer advice, and remind you that you're not alone in facing challenges. Reaching out to someone you trust and expressing your feelings can be incredibly cathartic. Whether it's a parent, sibling, or friend, sharing your worries can lighten the emotional load and provide new insights into your problems. Sometimes, just knowing someone is there for you is enough to ease the stress. It's about creating a circle of support where you can be both a giver and receiver of help, fostering deeper connections and mutual understanding.

*Interactive Element: Stress Management Reflection*

Consider taking a moment to reflect on your personal stress management strategies:

- Identify Your Stressors: Write down the top three sources of stress in your life.
- Explore Coping Mechanisms: Choose one new technique to try this week, such as journaling or meditation.
- Plan a Physical Activity: Schedule a specific time for a walk or other exercise each day.
- Strengthen Your Support Network: Reach out to a friend or family member this week for a chat or to share what's been on your mind.

Reflecting on these aspects can provide clarity and direction, helping you develop a personalized approach to managing stress effectively. By understanding your stressors and proactively addressing them, you can cultivate a more balanced and fulfilling life.

## 5.3 RECOGNIZING AND ADDRESSING MENTAL HEALTH ISSUES

In contemporary times, teens navigate a complex landscape of mental health challenges that significantly impact their daily experiences. The journey to understanding and addressing these challenges begins with identifying the most prevalent issues: anxiety and depression.

Anxiety typically manifests through persistent worry, restlessness, or difficulty concentrating, often leading to sensations of being on edge or experiencing an accelerated heart rate during mundane tasks. Conversely, depression might evoke persistent feelings of sadness, hopelessness, or disinterest in previously enjoyed activities, alongside alterations in sleep patterns and appetite. Early recognition of these symptoms, whether in oneself or others, is pivotal as they tend to remain under the radar until they escalate to overwhelming proportions.

Another significant concern is burnout, particularly prevalent among those balancing academic demands, extracurricular activities, and social commitments. Characterized by emotional, physical, and mental exhaustion from continuous stress, burnout can result in a sense of depletion and an inability to fulfill ongoing demands, diminishing motivation and performance.

Identifying these symptoms promptly may help resolve the issues before they progress any further, and can help provide timely access to necessary support and resources. If these situations progress to the point where they interfere with normal day-to-day activities, it might be time to look into additional help. The pursuit of skilled assistance is a critical measure when mental health challenges impede one's ability to function daily. Discerning the appropriate moment to seek help is essential. School counselors often serve as an accessible, initial support system, offering a nurturing space to voice concerns as well as guidance or referrals to therapists. Therapists are adept at aiding individuals through diverse techniques and therapies tailored to navigate mental health challenges.

Although initiating an appointment may seem intimidating, the process is relatively straightforward. Begin by identifying professionals within your insurance network or through school-provided resources. Contacting their office via phone or email will initiate the process of scheduling an appointment. It's important to understand that seeking assistance signifies a courageous and proactive step toward your well-being.

Incorporating daily self-care practices is instrumental in bolstering mental health. Establishing and maintaining a consistent sleep schedule is among the most efficacious strategies. Sleep serves as a restorative mechanism, crucial for mental acuity and emotional equilibrium. Striving for 7–9 hours of sleep nightly and adhering to consistent sleep and wake times aids in regulating the body's internal clock, thereby enhancing mood and concentration. Moreover, engaging in creative pursuits offers a valuable outlet for emotional expression and stress relief. Activities such as painting, writing, playing music, or crafting create a space for personal expression and relaxation, affording a reprieve from daily pressures and an opportunity to rejuvenate and reconnect with oneself. Embedding these practices into your daily regimen fortifies resilience and emotional health, rendering challenges more manageable.

Demystifying the stigma surrounding mental health is paramount in cultivating an environment conducive to open dialogue. This endeavor begins with sharing personal experiences with trusted confidants, nurturing understanding and empathy. Discussing one's mental health journey contributes to normalizing such conversations, diminishing the uncomfortable nature frequently associated with these topics. This transparency can motivate others to share their narratives, fostering a supportive community atmosphere. By engaging in open discourse, we collectively endorse a culture that prioritizes mental health on par with physical health, acknowledging that encountering mental health challenges is an intrinsic aspect of the human experience, and seeking assistance exemplifies strength rather than weakness. Encouraging candid conversations and offering support to others can dismantle barriers, engendering a more inclusive and empathetic society.

As this chapter concludes, it is vital to remember that mental health is an essential component of overall well-being. Acknowledging challenges, seeking help, engaging in self-care, and challenging stigma represent fundamental steps toward cultivating a healthier mental state. In the subsequent chapter, we delve into the pivotal role of technology and digital environments in contemporary life, providing insights on navigating these domains effectively.

# 6

# NAVIGATING TECHNOLOGY AND DIGITAL SPACES

*"In a digital world, clarity and humanity are key."*

— UNKNOWN

Imagine scrolling through your social media feed, where every post and message marks your digital footprint permanently. In this interconnected world, understanding digital etiquette is crucial. Just like in face-to-face interactions, online communication requires respect and awareness. Digital etiquette, often called "netiquette," is about maintaining a positive and respectful online presence. It guides how you interact with others, ensuring that your digital footprint reflects well on you. This is vital because the internet remembers everything. Every post, comment, and message contributes to your public image, impacting future opportunities. Good digital etiquette protects your privacy, prevents misunderstandings, and fosters a respectful online environment.

Using appropriate language and tone is fundamental in emails and messages. Just as yelling in a crowded room is frowned upon, typing in all caps in an email or text can be interpreted as shouting. It's crucial to remember that the absence of vocal tone and body language in digital communication can lead to misinterpretation. Therefore, clarity is critical. Choose words that convey your message accurately and respectfully. Avoid sarcasm or jokes that might be misunderstood without the context of your voice or expression. The goal is to communicate as clearly and thoughtfully as you would in person, allowing your message to be received as intended.

Structure is everything when it comes to crafting professional emails and messages. A well-organized email begins with a polite greeting, followed by a clear and concise body, and concludes with a courteous closing. Start with a simple greeting like "Dear" or "Hello," followed by the recipient's name. The body of your email should be direct and to the point, using paragraphs to separate different ideas. Avoid using slang or overly casual language, especially in professional settings. Before hitting send, take a moment to proofread for grammar and clarity. This ensures that your message is error-free and shows attention to detail and professionalism. A closing, such as "Best regards" or "Sincerely," followed by your name, rounds off your email, leaving a positive impression.

Miscommunications are inevitable in digital interactions, but they can be managed effectively. When misunderstandings arise, the first step is to seek clarification rather than make assumptions. For instance, avoid jumping to conclusions if a message seems curt or unclear. Instead, ask questions to understand the sender's intent. Phrases like "Could you clarify what you meant by..." or "I'm not sure I understand..." invite open dialogue and prevent further confusion. This approach resolves misunderstandings and demonstrates your willingness to communicate openly and respectfully.

Respecting privacy and boundaries in digital spaces is essential for maintaining trust and positive relationships. As mentioned, always seek their permission before tagging friends in photos or sharing personal information. This simple act acknowledges their right to control what appears on their public profiles. Understand that everyone has different comfort levels regarding their online presence, and it's important to honor those boundaries. Respecting privacy extends to avoiding over-sharing or posting sensitive information without consent. By practicing these principles, you contribute to a digital environment that values respect and consideration for others.

***Interactive Element: Email Composition Exercise***

To practice crafting professional emails, try this exercise:

- **Scenario:** Imagine you must request a meeting with your teacher to discuss an assignment.
- **Compose Your Email:**
    - **Greeting:** Start with a respectful salutation.
    - **Body:** Clearly state the purpose of your email, including specific questions or topics you wish to discuss.
    - **Closing:** End with a polite closing and your name.
- **Proofread:** Check for spelling and grammar errors before sending.

This exercise can enhance your email-writing skills and ensure clear and professional digital communication. Practicing these elements will prepare you for effective interactions in academic and professional settings.

## 6.1 MANAGING SCREEN TIME FOR BETTER BALANCE

In a world where screens captivate our attention from dawn to dusk, it's essential to understand their effects on our well-being. Excessive screen time can disrupt sleep patterns, making it difficult to fall asleep and stay asleep. The blue light emitted by screens suppresses melatonin, the hormone responsible for regulating sleep. This disruption can lead to fatigue, irritability, and difficulty concentrating. Besides affecting sleep, prolonged screen exposure increases the risk of eye strain, characterized by headaches, blurred vision, and dry eyes. The constant focus on digital devices demands a lot from our eyes, and proper care is necessary to avoid discomfort and decreased productivity. Recognizing these impacts is the first step toward mitigating them and finding a healthier balance.

Setting limits on screen time can be a game-changer in maintaining both physical and mental health. Technology offers tools to help manage usage effectively. Apps designed to track and restrict screen time can be invaluable. These apps monitor your time on various activities, allowing you to set daily or weekly limits for different categories. For instance, you could limit social media use to one hour a day. Doing so creates boundaries that encourage you to engage in other activities. This conscious regulation of screen time fosters a balanced lifestyle, ensuring that digital interactions don't overshadow the offline experiences that enrich your life.

Creating a balanced daily routine involves more than just cutting back on screen time; it's about filling those hours with meaningful activities. Start by structuring your day to include non-digital pursuits. Allocate specific times for outdoor activities, like a morning jog or an afternoon walk. Physical activity boosts your mood and gives your eyes a much-needed break from screens. Incorporate hobbies such as reading, drawing, or playing a musical instrument. These activities stimulate creativity and provide a sense of accomplishment, offering a fulfilling alternative to endless scrolling. By establishing a routine prioritizing physical and mental engagement, you cultivate a lifestyle that values real-world connections and experiences.

Mindful media consumption is another vital component of managing screen time. In an era where information is abundant, it's crucial to critically evaluate the content you consume. Start by questioning the credibility of online sources. Is the information coming from a reputable outlet or an unknown website? Reliable sources often have a track record of accuracy and transparency. Check the author's credentials and look for citations or references. This scrutiny helps you distinguish between factual content and misinformation. By approaching digital content with a discerning eye, you protect yourself from false narratives and develop a more informed perspective on the world around you.

***Interactive Element: Screen Time Reflection Exercise***

Take a moment to evaluate your screen time habits by reflecting on the following prompts:

- **Daily Usage:** How much time do you spend on screens daily? Consider tracking this using a screen time app for a week.

- **Alternative Activities:** List three non-digital activities you enjoy or want to try. How can you incorporate these into your daily routine?
- **Content Evaluation:** Identify a recent article or video you consumed. Do you know if it was from a credible source? What criteria did you use to determine its validity?

You can use this exercise to gain insight into your digital habits and explore ways to balance screen time with enriching offline experiences. This reflection encourages mindful engagement with technology, promoting a healthier relationship with the digital world.

## 6.2 PROTECTING PERSONAL INFORMATION ONLINE

Understanding data privacy is crucial in the vast digital landscape where every click can leave a trace. Data privacy refers to protecting personal information from unauthorized access or exposure. Sharing personal data publicly, such as your location, contact details, or even your birthday, carries significant risks. Identity thieves can misuse this information to impersonate you or gain access to your financial accounts. Once your personal data is out in the open, retrieving it is nearly impossible, making it essential to be cautious about what you share online. Protecting your information isn't just about keeping your secrets; it's about maintaining control over your identity and minimizing vulnerabilities.

Creating strong, secure passwords is one of the simplest yet most effective ways to protect your personal information. A good password acts as a barrier against unauthorized access to your accounts. To craft a strong password, use a mix of uppercase and lowercase letters, numbers, and symbols. The longer the password, the better. Avoid obvious choices like birthdays or simple sequences like "123456." Instead, consider using a password manager, a tool that generates and stores complex passwords for you. This enhances security and saves you from the hassle of remembering multiple passwords. Regularly updating your passwords further bolsters your defenses against potential breaches.

Phishing and scams are lurking threats in the digital world, designed to trick you into revealing sensitive information. Phishing often involves emails that appear to be from legitimate sources, like your bank or a popular website, asking you to verify your account details. To spot these fraudulent emails, carefully examine the sender's address for any inconsistencies or typos that might indicate it's not authentic. Another red flag is suspicious links; always hover over a link to see where it leads before clicking. If something feels off, trust your instincts and avoid engaging with the email. These scams prey on trust and urgency, so verifying authenticity can save you from falling victim.

Adjusting privacy settings on social media platforms is a proactive step in safeguarding your personal information. These settings control who can see your posts, photos, and personal details. Limiting your profile visibility to friends only is a good start. This ensures that only people you know and trust can access your information. Regularly reviewing and updating these settings is important, as platforms often change their privacy policies or introduce new features. Additionally, be mindful of third-party apps connected to your accounts, as they might have access to more information than necessary. By actively managing your privacy settings, you maintain greater control over your digital presence, reducing the risk of unwanted exposure.

## 6.3 IDENTIFYING AND RESPONDING TO CYBERBULLYING

In the vast world of digital interactions, cyberbullying remains a pressing concern, often hidden behind screens and anonymous profiles. Recognizing the signs of cyberbullying is the first step in addressing it. Harassing messages or comments can take many forms, from cruel jokes to aggressive threats, often leaving the victim feeling isolated and vulnerable. Exclusion from online groups is another tactic, where individuals are intentionally left out of chats or social media circles, leading to feelings of alienation. These acts might seem subtle, but they can have profound effects on a person's mental well-being. Understanding these signs is crucial for both identifying and supporting those who may be suffering silently.

When faced with cyberbullying, taking decisive action is key. Documenting evidence is an essential first step, as it records the interactions. This can be done by taking screenshots of harmful messages, comments, or posts. Having this evidence is vital when reporting incidents to platform moderators, who can take appropriate action against the offenders. Most social media platforms have reporting tools designed to handle such situations, ensuring that harmful content is removed and that users who violate community guidelines face consequences. By using these tools, you contribute to making digital spaces safer for everyone.

Seeking support is crucial when dealing with cyberbullying. It's important to reach out to trusted adults, such as parents, teachers, or school counselors, who can provide guidance and assistance. They can help navigate the situation, offering advice on how to proceed and ensuring that you're not facing it alone. Support services and hotlines are also available, providing professional advice and a listening ear for those who need it. Remember, reaching out for help is a sign of strength, not weakness. It's about building a support network that empowers you to tackle challenges head-on.

Creating a safe online environment requires collective effort. Promoting kindness and respect in online interactions is a powerful way to combat cyberbullying. This means being mindful of the impact your words can have on others and choosing to uplift rather than tear down. Encouraging positive behavior online can inspire others to do the same, creating a ripple effect that fosters a supportive digital community. Share messages of encouragement, and stand up against negativity when you see it. By actively participating in creating a respectful online space, you contribute to a culture where everyone feels valued and safe.

*Reflection Section: Cyberbullying Awareness*

Take a moment to reflect on your awareness and readiness to handle cyberbullying:

- **Recognizing Signs:** Have you noticed any signs of cyberbullying in your digital interactions? How did it make you feel?
- **Action Steps:** Consider how you might document and report cyberbullying if you encounter it. What steps would you take?
- **Support Network:** Identify trusted adults or resources you could turn to for help and guidance.
- **Promoting Positivity:** Think about ways you can contribute to a safe and respectful online environment. How can you encourage others to do the same?

This reflection encourages a proactive approach to cyberbullying, empowering you to recognize, respond, and create a positive digital presence. By being informed and prepared, you can navigate the digital world with confidence and resilience.

## 6.4 USING TECHNOLOGY FOR EDUCATIONAL SUCCESS

In today's digital age, technology opens doors to endless learning opportunities. Online tools and platforms have revolutionized how we approach education, making it more accessible and engaging than ever before. One of the standout resources is Khan Academy, which offers various supplementary lessons across multiple subjects. Whether struggling with algebra or curious about world history, Khan Academy provides clear, interactive lessons catering to different learning styles. The platform is free and accessible, making it a valuable asset for students seeking to deepen their understanding outside the classroom. Additionally, the availability of e-books and academic journals online means you have a library ready to support your studies with credible information and insights.

Organizational tools and apps can transform how you manage your academic responsibilities. Google Calendar, for example, is an excellent tool for planning and organizing your study schedule. It allows you to set reminders for assignments, exams, and important deadlines, ensuring nothing slips through the cracks. By visually mapping out your week, you gain a clearer picture of your commitments and can allocate time accordingly. This improves your time management and reduces stress by keeping you on track. There are also apps like Evernote and Todoist, which help you organize notes and tasks in one convenient place. These tools encourage you to structure your academic life efficiently, freeing up mental space to focus on learning.

Developing strong digital research skills is essential in navigating the vast ocean of information available online. The key to successful research lies in distinguishing credible sources from unreliable ones. Start by evaluating the author's credentials and the publication's reputation. Peer-reviewed journals, government websites, and established educational institutions are generally trustworthy. Be wary of blogs or opinion pieces without citations or references. Cross-referencing information from multiple sources can also help verify accuracy. Ethical research goes beyond just finding information; it involves giving credit where it's due. Always cite your sources to acknowledge the original authors and avoid plagiarism. By honing these skills, you become a more informed and responsible learner, capable of navigating the digital landscape with confidence.

Balancing technology use in education involves integrating digital tools with traditional study methods to maximize learning. While technology offers interactive and immediate access to information, traditional methods like handwritten notes or physical textbooks still hold value. Studies have shown that handwritten notes can enhance memory retention, providing a tactile connection to the material. Consider blending both approaches—use online platforms for research and interactive exercises, but take notes by hand during lectures or while reading. This combination allows you to leverage the strengths of both methods, creating a more holistic learning experience. It's about finding what works best for you and using technology as a tool to complement, rather than replace, traditional learning practices.

As we wrap up this chapter, it's clear that technology, when used thoughtfully, can significantly enhance educational experiences. By leveraging online resources, organizing effectively, conducting ethical research, and balancing digital with traditional methods, you equip yourself with a robust set of skills for academic success.

These practices prepare you for school and lifelong learning and adaptability in an ever-evolving world. Next, we'll explore how these skills translate into real-world scenarios, setting the stage for your continued growth.

# 7

# EDUCATIONAL AND CAREER PLANNING

*"Choose a job you love, and you will never have to work a day in your life."*

— CONFUCIUS

Imagine standing at a crossroad with multiple paths stretching before you, each representing a different future. The choices you make now will shape the trajectory of your academic and career journey. Setting clear and achievable goals is like having a map that guides you through this complex landscape. It transforms abstract aspirations into tangible milestones, providing direction and motivation. Setting goals creates a blueprint for your ambitions, helping you stay focused and committed to your path, even when distractions and challenges arise. Understanding the importance of goal setting is crucial. It's not just about dreaming big; it's about charting a course and taking the necessary steps to reach your destination.

When discussing goals, it's essential to differentiate between short-term and long-term objectives. Short-term goals act as stepping stones, leading you toward broader, long-term aspirations. For instance, if your ultimate aim is to become a doctor, a short-term goal might be excelling in your science classes this semester. These smaller targets keep you engaged and provide regular satisfaction as you tick them off your list. Long-term goals, on the other hand, require more time and sustained effort. They provide a vision of your future, motivating you to persevere through challenges. Balancing both types of goals ensures you're making consistent progress while keeping your eyes on the bigger picture.

A practical way to set effective goals is by using the SMART criteria, which stands for Specific, Measurable, Achievable, Relevant, and Time-bound. SMART goals help clarify your objectives and outline a clear path to achieve them. For example, instead of vaguely aiming to "do better in math," you might set a goal to raise your math grade from a B to an A by the end of the semester. This goal is specific (improving your math grade), measurable (from a B to an A), achievable (with the right effort and resources), relevant (important for academic success), and time-bound (by the end of the semester). SMART goals transform your aspirations into actionable plans, making tracking progress and staying motivated easier.

Another powerful tool for staying focused is creating a personal vision board. This visual representation of your goals constantly reminds you of what you're working toward. Gather magazine cutouts, quotes, and images that resonate with your ambitions and arrange them on a board. Place it somewhere you'll see daily, like your bedroom wall or study area. Each time you glance at it, you reinforce your commitment to your goals and visualize your future success. A vision board inspires and helps maintain clarity and motivation, especially on days when motivation wanes.

Regularly reviewing and adjusting your goals is essential for maintaining momentum. Life is dynamic, and circumstances change, so it's important to remain flexible. Set monthly check-ins to evaluate your progress and make adjustments as needed. During these check-ins, reflect on what's working and what's not. Are you on track to achieve your goals, or do you need to modify your approach? This reflection helps you stay aligned with your objectives and make informed decisions about your path forward. It's about being proactive and adaptable, ensuring that your goals remain relevant and achievable as you grow and evolve.

***Interactive Element: Goal Setting Reflection***

To enhance your goal-setting process, try this reflection exercise:

- **Identify a Long-Term Goal:** Write down a long-term aspiration and break it into smaller, short-term goals.
- **Apply the SMART Criteria:** Choose one short-term goal and ensure it meets the SMART criteria.
- **Create a Vision Board:** Gather images and quotes representing your goals and arrange them on a board.
- **Set a Monthly Check-In:** Schedule a monthly date to review your progress and adjust your goals as needed.

Use this exercise to refine your goals and stay motivated on your academic and career journey. By regularly engaging with your goals, you cultivate a sense of purpose and direction, empowering you to succeed.

## 7.1 EFFECTIVE STUDY HABITS AND TIME MANAGEMENT

Establishing a study routine can be a game-changer in your academic journey. It's about finding and sticking to a rhythm that suits your lifestyle. Start by identifying the times of day when you feel most alert and focused, and allocate these periods for studying. Maybe you're a morning person who thrives before lunch, or perhaps your energy peaks in the evening. Once you've pinpointed these windows, dedicate specific times for each subject. Using a planner or calendar can help organize these sessions, providing a visual layout of your week. A structured schedule prevents the last-minute cramming that often leads to stress and burnout, allowing you to approach your studies calmly and clearly.

Regarding focused studying, techniques like the Pomodoro Technique can enhance concentration and retention. This method involves working in short, intense bursts—typically 25 minutes—followed by a five-minute break. This approach capitalizes on the brain's ability to focus better in shorter, concentrated intervals. Active recall is another powerful tool for testing the material, reinforcing learning through retrieval practice. Combine this with spaced repetition, which involves revisiting the material at increasing intervals to improve memory retention. These strategies work together to solidify knowledge, turning study sessions into efficient and productive experiences.

Balancing schoolwork with extracurricular activities requires careful planning and prioritization. Begin by listing all your commitments, both academic and extracurricular. Use a to-do list to prioritize tasks, distinguishing between urgent and less critical activities. This helps ensure that essential responsibilities are met without feeling overwhelmed. Allocating specific time slots for each activity can prevent overlap and reduce stress. Remember, it's about quality, not quantity—focusing on key tasks rather than spreading yourself too thin. This balance allows you to engage in extracurriculars you're passionate about while maintaining academic excellence.

Procrastination is a common hurdle in academic pursuits, but breaking tasks into smaller, manageable steps can help overcome it. Instead of viewing a large project as a daunting task, divide it into smaller sections and tackle each one individually. This approach makes the workload feel more manageable and encourages progress. Setting deadlines for each stage of a project provides structure and accountability, motivating you to stay on track. The satisfaction of completing each step fuels momentum, gradually leading to the successful completion of the entire task. This technique enhances productivity and builds confidence in your ability to manage complex assignments.

*Interactive Element: Study Routine Planner*

To put these strategies into practice, try creating a study routine planner:

- **Identify Your Peak Focus Times:** Reflect on when you feel most alert and assign these times for studying.
- **Allocate Study Sessions:** Use a calendar to block specific times for each subject.
- **Incorporate Breaks:** Plan short breaks using the Pomodoro Technique.
- **Create a To-Do List:** Prioritize tasks by urgency and importance.
- **Set Mini-Deadlines:** Break projects into stages with specific deadlines.

This planner helps you establish a consistent routine, enhancing focus and time management. By organizing your study schedule, you gain control over your academic responsibilities, paving the way for success.

## 7.2 EXPLORING HIGHER EDUCATION OPTIONS

Choosing the right path after high school can seem like navigating a maze with endless turns. A solid starting point is to gain a clear understanding of the various higher education options available. Traditional universities, for instance, offer expansive curriculums that allow for comprehensive study in specialized areas over four-year periods. These institutions are known for their vibrant campus life, brimming with a variety of activities, clubs, and resources designed to enrich the student experience. On the flip side, community colleges present a cost-effective alternative, providing two-year associate degrees. This route is particularly beneficial for those looking to complete general education requirements before making a financial and time commitment to a four-year university, thus allowing a seamless transition without compromising on education quality.

For individuals drawn to specific trades, vocational schools offer practical, hands-on training in fields such as plumbing, electrical work, or cosmetology. These programs are usually shorter, directly preparing students for immediate entry into the workforce. Each educational path caters to unique preferences, career objectives, and learning styles, making it crucial to reflect on what best matches your goals and way of learning.

After pinpointing the type of institution that resonates with your goals, the next pivotal step is to delve into potential majors and career paths. This stage can often feel intimidating, yet aligning your academic pursuits with your interests and envisioned career trajectory is critical. A practical approach to untangling this confusion is to engage with career assessment tools. These tools are helpful in uncovering your strengths and pinpointing interests, potentially revealing exciting fields you might not have initially considered. Complementing this, conducting informational interviews with professionals in fields that spark your curiosity can shed light on the realities of daily job responsibilities, challenges encountered, and the satisfaction derived from their work. Such direct insights can be incredibly enlightening, offering a deeper understanding that is more in-depth than the generic overviews found in promotional materials or online research. This blend of self-assessment and real-world exploration can be instrumental in guiding your decision-making process regarding your major and future career path.

Financing your education is another critical aspect to consider. Financial aid and scholarships can make a significant difference, turning your educational aspirations into reality. Start by accurately completing the Free Application for Federal Student Aid (FAFSA), which determines your eligibility for federal grants, loans, and work-study programs. This is a crucial step, as many scholarships also require FAFSA completion. You can also search for scholarships specific to your interests, background, or intended field of study. Many organizations offer financial awards for students who are planning to pursue a career or for those who excel in certain areas. Applying for multiple scholarships increases your chances of receiving aid, easing the financial burden of higher education.

Visiting campuses can provide a deeper understanding of life as a student at each institution. Virtual tours are an excellent alternative if visiting in person isn't possible, offering a glimpse into the campus environment and facilities. Prepare questions to ask during these tours, such as inquiries about student support services, extracurricular activities, and campus amenities. Comparing these aspects can help you determine which institution aligns with your personal and academic needs. It's about finding a place where you feel comfortable and supported, ensuring that your educational experience is both fulfilling and conducive to your growth.

## 7.3 WRITING A PROFESSIONAL RESUME AND COVER LETTER

Creating a professional resume is one of the first steps in presenting yourself to potential employers. It's your personal marketing document, highlighting what makes you a valuable candidate. A strong resume begins with your contact information, placed at the top, so employers can easily reach you. Include your full name, phone number, email address, and LinkedIn profile if applicable. Following this, your education section should list your school, expected graduation date, and any relevant coursework or honors. Next, outline your skills and experience, focusing on those that align with the job you're applying for. Use action verbs to describe your achievements, such as "developed," "managed," or "improved," to convey a sense of initiative and impact. These details create a dynamic picture of your capabilities, making your resume more compelling to those skimming through multiple applications.

Tailoring your resume for each job application is crucial. Each position may value different skills and experiences, so customizing your resume to match the job description can set you apart from the competition. Highlight the most relevant aspects of your background, ensuring they align with the requirements of the role. For instance, if you're applying for a marketing internship, emphasize any related coursework, projects, or extracurricular activities that showcase your skills in this area. This targeted approach shows employers that you've done your homework and understand how your abilities can benefit their organization. It also increases the chances of your resume making it past initial screenings, landing you an interview where you can further demonstrate your suitability.

A cover letter complements your resume, providing a more detailed narrative of your qualifications and enthusiasm for the role. Begin by addressing the letter to a specific person whenever possible, as this personal touch can make your application stand out. Research the company and mention specific details about its mission or recent projects to demonstrate your interest and knowledge. Explain why you are well-suited for the position, linking your experiences and skills to the company's needs. This is your opportunity to show how your background and aspirations align with the company's goals, making you a valuable addition to their team. A compelling cover letter should be concise yet impactful, leaving a lasting impression on the reader.

Avoiding common mistakes in resumes and cover letters can significantly enhance their effectiveness. Generic language and clichés often plague these documents, reducing their impact. Phrases like "hard worker" or "team player" are overused and offer little substance. Instead, provide specific examples that illustrate these qualities, such as detailing a time when you led a successful team project. Additionally, proofreading is paramount. Typos and grammatical errors can undermine your professionalism, suggesting a lack of attention to detail. Carefully review your documents or ask a trusted friend to ensure they are polished and error-free before submission. This meticulousness reflects your commitment to presenting yourself in the best possible light.

## 7.4 PREPARING FOR JOB INTERVIEWS WITH CONFIDENCE

Approaching a job interview can feel like stepping into the spotlight, with all eyes on you. But preparation is your best ally in transforming nerves into confidence. One of the most impactful ways to prepare is by researching the company and the role you're applying for. Delve into the company's mission and values to understand its culture and goals. This knowledge helps you tailor your responses and demonstrates genuine interest in the organization. Familiarize yourself with recent company news or projects, as these can be excellent talking points during your interview. Highlighting your awareness of the company's achievements shows that you're proactive and informed, qualities that any employer would value.

Once you've immersed yourself in the company's world, it's time to practice common interview questions. "Tell me about yourself" is often the opener, and a concise yet engaging response is key. Focus on relevant experiences and skills, and structure your answer to flow naturally. Think of it as your personal elevator pitch. The STAR method—Situation, Task, Action, Result—can be incredibly helpful for behavioral questions. This technique involves describing a specific situation, the task you were faced with, the action you took, and the result of your efforts. It's a structured way to showcase your problem-solving abilities and achievements, leaving a lasting impression on your interviewer.

Non-verbal communication plays a crucial role in how you're perceived during an interview. Your body language can speak volumes before you even utter a word. Maintain eye contact to convey confidence and engagement. It shows that you're attentive and genuinely interested in the conversation. A confident posture —sitting up straight with shoulders back—projects self-assurance.

Avoid crossing your arms, as this can appear defensive. Dressing appropriately is also vital. Your attire should reflect the company's culture while maintaining professionalism. A polished appearance demonstrates respect for the opportunity and attention to detail, both of which can make a positive impact.

After the interview, sending a thank-you note is more than just a formality—it's an opportunity to reinforce your interest and leave a lasting impression. Craft a thoughtful follow-up email that expresses gratitude for the opportunity to interview. Mention specific points from the conversation that resonated with you, and reiterate your enthusiasm for the role. This shows professionalism and keeps you top of mind as the hiring team makes their decision. A well-crafted thank-you note can set you apart from other candidates, highlighting your communication skills and appreciation for the opportunity.

## 7.5 EXPLORING DIFFERENT CAREER PATHS

Picture yourself standing at a crossroads, each path leading to a different future. This is what choosing a career path often feels like. The first step in navigating these choices is identifying your personal interests and strengths. Take a moment to reflect on the activities you naturally gravitate towards—perhaps it's writing, solving puzzles, or helping others. These hobbies and interests often explain the fields where you might excel. To gain more precise insights, consider taking career aptitude tests. These assessments evaluate your skills, preferences, and values, helping you understand which careers align with your natural talents and passions. You can find these tests online or your guidance counselor may have some they can recommend. Reflecting on these results can illuminate potential paths you hadn't considered, guiding you toward roles where you can thrive.

Once you have an idea of your interests, it's time to research the career options out there. The world of work is vast and ever-evolving, with countless opportunities across various industries. Online platforms like O*NET and CareerOneStop are invaluable resources. They provide detailed information about different professions, including job responsibilities, necessary skills, and future outlook. Spend some time exploring these sites to learn about the roles that pique your interest. Understanding the requirements and expectations of potential careers can help you make informed decisions about your education and skill development. Armed with this knowledge, you can begin to chart a course that aligns with your interests and the job market demands.

Gaining practical experience is a crucial step in exploring career options. Internships and volunteering offer firsthand insight into specific fields, allowing you to test the waters before diving in. High school students can apply for internships in areas that align with their interests, gaining valuable experience and networking opportunities. Volunteering at local organizations is another excellent way to immerse yourself in a field. Whether it's helping at a community center or assisting in a business environment, volunteering provides practical exposure and enhances your resume. These experiences build skills and confirm whether a particular career is the right fit for you. They offer a glimpse into the day-to-day realities of a job, helping you make more informed career decisions.

Networking plays a pivotal role in building a successful career. It's about creating connections and opening doors to opportunities that might otherwise remain closed. Start by attending career fairs and industry events, where you can meet professionals from various fields. These interactions are more than just exchanges of business cards; they are opportunities to learn from those who have walked the path before you. Informational interviews are another valuable tool. Reach out to professionals in careers that interest you and ask for a brief meeting to learn about their experiences. These conversations can provide insights that no online resource can offer, giving you a deeper understanding of the industry and potential career paths. Building a network of contacts can provide guidance, job leads, and mentorship, all of which are invaluable as you begin your career journey.

In this chapter, we've explored how to align your interests and strengths with potential career paths, the importance of research and practical experience, and the value of networking. As you ponder these insights, remember that your career is a journey of exploration and growth. With thoughtful reflection and proactive steps, you can forge a fulfilling and successful path. Your decision now is a step towards a future that reflects your ambitions and passions.

# 8

# INDEPENDENT LIVING SKILLS

*"Independence is not a destination, it's a journey."*

— UNKNOWN

Picture this: it's Saturday afternoon, and you're home alone when suddenly, the kitchen sink starts leaking. Water pools on the floor, and panic sets in. You realize you've never dealt with something like this before. As you scramble to find a solution, it becomes clear why knowing basic home maintenance skills is crucial. These skills are more than just handy tricks—they're essential for maintaining your living space, ensuring safety, and even saving money on professional repairs. Mastering these basics gives you the confidence to tackle everyday challenges, transforming potential crises into manageable tasks.

## 8.1 ESSENTIAL HOME MAINTENANCE SKILLS

Let's talk about the basic tool kit essentials every home should have. Imagine them as your personal set of superheroes, ready to save the day when things go awry. A hammer, screwdrivers, and pliers are your foundational trio. The hammer helps with everything from hanging pictures to assembling furniture. Screwdrivers —both flathead and Phillips—are crucial for tightening or loosening screws. Pliers grip, twist, and cut wires, making them indispensable for minor fixes. Alongside these, a tape measure and level ensure precision, whether you're hanging shelves or measuring for curtains. A utility knife easily slices through boxes and trims materials, while an adjustable wrench tackles nuts and bolts, allowing you to fix leaky faucets or assemble equipment.

Performing simple repairs is the next step in building your independent living skills. Let's revisit that leaky faucet scenario. Often, the culprit is a worn-out washer. With the right tools and a new washer, you can unscrew the faucet, replace the faulty part, and reassemble it, stopping the leak at its source. Another common household issue is a clogged sink. Here, a plunger becomes your best friend. Creating a seal and applying steady pressure can dislodge the obstruction, restoring normal flow. These tasks may seem intimidating initially, but with patience and practice, they become straightforward. They save you the cost of hiring a professional and give you a sense of accomplishment and control over your environment.

Regular seasonal home maintenance checks prevent more significant issues and maintain efficiency. Start with checking smoke detector batteries. This simple act ensures your home is safe and compliant with safety standards. Next, focus on your air conditioning filters. Over time, they accumulate dust and dirt, hampering performance and air quality. Regular cleaning or replacement keeps your system running smoothly and your air fresh. These tasks are often overlooked, but they play a vital role in home upkeep, preventing more significant problems down the line and ensuring your living space remains comfortable and secure.

While many tasks can be handled with basic skills and tools, it's crucial to recognize when to call a professional. Electrical wiring issues, for example, pose significant risks if not addressed by experts. Similarly, major plumbing leaks require specialized knowledge and tools. Attempting to fix these yourself can lead to further damage or even danger. Knowing your limits is a vital part of home maintenance. It ensures that you tackle what you can and seek help when necessary, maintaining a balance between independence and safety.

*Interactive Element: Home Maintenance Checklist*

To keep track of these tasks, consider creating a home maintenance checklist. List the essential tools you need and common repairs you might encounter. Schedule seasonal checks like smoke detector testing and filter cleaning. This checklist organizes your maintenance efforts and serves as a guide, helping you build confidence in your abilities while ensuring your home remains a safe and well-maintained haven.

The ability to perform basic home maintenance tasks empowers you to navigate the challenges of independent living confidently. It's about taking control of your environment and ensuring your home is a place of safety and comfort.

## 8.2 UNDERSTANDING NUTRITION AND MEAL PLANNING

Imagine yourself opening the refrigerator and instantly knowing which ingredients to combine for dinner, guided not just by a preset plan but by an understanding of your body's nutritional needs. This scenario underscores that nutrition is more important than mere food consumption; it involves nourishing your body with the essential elements it requires to thrive. A well-balanced diet is foundational, comprising proteins, carbohydrates, and fats, each serving a unique yet pivotal function. Proteins, the building blocks of your muscles and tissues, are crucial for repair and growth. Carbohydrates are your body's main energy source, fueling you through academic challenges and physical activities alike. Fats, often unjustly vilified, play a critical role in nutrient absorption and cell growth. Beyond these macronutrients, vitamins and minerals, though they do not contribute calories, significantly impact bodily functions such as immune defense and bone strength, highlighting their indispensable roles in maintaining health.

Navigating the grocery aisles becomes an exercise in informed decision-making when you grasp the importance of understanding nutrition labels. These labels are windows into the contents of packaged foods, from the enticing cereal box to the health-branded snack bars. Combining contents with the serving size can prevent unintentional overeating due to misleading portion indications. The next step involves scanning for added sugars and sodium levels, which can lurk in surprising quantities within products, posing long-term health risks. Recognizing these hidden components equips you with the knowledge to make food selections that align with your health objectives, so you choose indulgences judiciously rather than trying to eliminate them.

Embarking on the journey of meal planning is less about culinary expertise or dedicating excessive time to food preparation and more about planning in alignment with your lifestyle and financial situation. Start with devising a weekly meal plan that embraces a variety of food groups, guaranteeing a spectrum of nutrients. Visualize plates bursting with color from an assortment of vegetables, complemented by lean proteins, whole grains, and beneficial fats. Simple, nourishing recipes such as a vibrant vegetable stir-fry or a soul-warming lentil soup can become staples in your diet. These dishes not only provide essential nutrients but also contribute to financial savings by curtailing spontaneous food purchases. Cooking at home affords you the autonomy to manage ingredients, adjust portion sizes, and cater to your taste preferences, transforming healthy eating into a pleasurable and sustainable practice.

Mindful eating introduces an additional dimension to your dietary habits. This practice is more than just the act of eating, focusing instead on how you engage with food. It involves attuning to your body's hunger signals, distinguishing genuine hunger from emotional eating or eating out of boredom. Picture yourself fully enjoying the experience of eating, savoring every mouthful, and relishing the textures and flavors. Such mindfulness enhances digestive efficiency and satisfaction, diminishing the desire for overconsumption. Cultivating a mindful approach to eating encourages a harmonious relationship with food, where meals are savored as sources of nourishment and joy rather than eliciting feelings of stress or guilt.

*Interactive Element: Meal Planning Reflection*

Take a moment to reflect on your current eating habits. Consider what changes you might make to align better with the principles of balanced nutrition and mindful eating:

- List your favorite meals and identify which food groups they include.
- Reflect on your grocery shopping habits. Do you check nutrition labels?
- Plan one balanced meal for the week, focusing on diverse nutrients.
- Practice mindful eating during one meal, noting how it impacts your enjoyment and satisfaction.

This reflection encourages a deeper understanding of your nutrition habits and helps develop a plan that suits your needs and goals.

## 8.3 BASIC COOKING TECHNIQUES FOR BEGINNERS

Embarking on your first culinary journey can feel like navigating uncharted territory. However, acquainting yourself with a handful of essential cooking techniques paves the way for a lifetime of kitchen triumphs. The art of boiling, steaming, and sautéing constitutes the bedrock of cooking mastery. Boiling involves bringing water to a vigorous, bubbling state before introducing ingredients like pasta or vegetables, which guarantees even cooking throughout. Conversely, steaming employs the gentle caress of hot vapor to cook food, preserving its delicate nutrients and flavors—ideal for tender vegetables, succulent fish, and plump dumplings. Sautéing, on the other hand, demands a degree of skill, quick-cooking food in just a whisper of oil over medium-high flames to achieve a golden-brown exterior and depth of flavor. These fundamental techniques not only expand your culinary repertoire but also instill confidence with every dish prepared. Knife skills are a pivotal element of culinary proficiency. Efficient and safe food preparation begins with mastering the art of the blade. Initiate this journey by gripping the knife's handle firmly with your dominant hand, adopting a pinch grip for superior control. As you maneuver the blade, your non-dominant hand should adopt a 'claw' position, guiding food items safely and allowing for precise cuts. Embark on practicing with various foods —dicing onions, julienning bell peppers, and finely mincing garlic —to refine your technique. Remember, a sharp knife is your ally, demanding less force and mitigating the risk of accidents. Regular maintenance of your knife's edge ensures a safer, more pleasurable cooking experience.

The secret to spontaneous and inspired meal creation lies in a well-stocked pantry. Essential seasonings such as salt, pepper, and garlic powder lay the groundwork for enhancing the flavor profiles of countless dishes with minimal effort. Essentials like rice, pasta, and a selection of canned vegetables act as pillars for crafting quick, nutritious meals. Armed with these staples and a sprinkle of creativity, you can effortlessly conjure up dishes like a savory stir-fry, a robust pasta entrée, or a comforting vegetable soup, circumventing the need for last-minute grocery expeditions. A pantry brimming with possibilities not only offers convenience but also invites culinary creativity, enabling you to experiment with an array of flavors and textures without the confines of stringent recipes. The ability to follow a recipe with precision can transform a seemingly complex dish into a delightful culinary achievement. Begin this process by perusing the entire recipe, familiarizing yourself with its demands, and assembling all required ingredients. A keen eye for measurements and terminology is crucial—understanding the distinction between a tablespoon and a teaspoon could be the difference between success and mishap. The practice of mise en place, or preparing and measuring ingredients in advance, streamlines your cooking process, alleviating stress and allowing you to immerse fully in the art of cooking. This methodical approach elevates your kitchen efficiency and enhances the overall enjoyment of the cooking experience.

Prioritizing safety in the kitchen is indispensable. Employing oven mitts when handling hot items, such as baking trays or pots, safeguards against burns. Diligent storage of perishable items is essential to prevent spoilage and protect against foodborne illnesses. Prompt refrigeration of leftovers and ensuring raw meats are kept separate to prevent cross-contamination are critical practices. Adherence to these safety measures fosters a secure cooking environment, letting the joy and creativity of culinary exploration take center stage. Equipped with these foundational skills and safety precautions, you stand ready to embark on a confident and secure culinary adventure.

## 8.4 ORGANIZING AND DECLUTTERING YOUR SPACE

Picture yourself entering a room that is chaotic and cluttered. The sensation might be overwhelming, with stress levels rising as you struggle to focus. Now imagine the opposite: a tidy, organized space where everything has its place. This environment can do wonders for your mental well-being and productivity. A well-organized room reduces stress and anxiety by creating a sense of calm and order. It allows your mind to focus on the task at hand without the constant distraction of clutter. When your surroundings are neat, your mind is free to think clearly and efficiently, boosting your ability to concentrate and complete tasks with ease.

Finding the right decluttering techniques can transform your living space into a sanctuary. One popular method is the KonMari Method, which only keeps items that spark joy. This approach encourages you to evaluate each possession, asking yourself whether it genuinely adds value to your life. If it doesn't, it might be time to let it go. Pair this with creating a donation plan for unwanted items. Instead of tossing out belongings, consider donating them to local charities or community centers. This clears your space and benefits others who might find joy in what you no longer need. Decluttering becomes an act of giving, enriching your life and the lives of others.

Organizational tools and solutions are your allies to maintain order in various areas of the home. Storage bins and baskets can be used to group similar items, making them easy to find and reducing visual clutter. A quick trip to the dollar store can provide a reasonably priced collection of suitably sized containers, with and without lids. Labeling shelves and containers is another effective strategy. By clearly marking where items belong, you streamline the process of putting things away, ensuring that everything has a defined spot. This practice minimizes the time spent searching for misplaced items and encourages everyone in the household to maintain order. Imagine the satisfaction of instantly locating your favorite book or the charger that always seems to vanish just when you need it. These tools enhance tidiness and cultivate a sense of control over your environment.

Developing habits for a clutter-free home is essential to prevent mess from accumulating over time. One useful strategy is the "one in, one out" rule. For every new item you bring into your space, consider removing one that no longer serves a purpose. This rule helps maintain balance and prevents over-accumulation. Setting aside time weekly for tidying up is another habit that keeps clutter at bay. Dedicate a specific day or time to reset your space, ensuring it remains organized and functional. This doesn't have to be daunting; even a short session can make a significant difference. Regular tidying fosters a routine that, over time, becomes second nature, promoting a consistently organized environment.

**Reflection Section: Decluttering Journal**

Consider starting a decluttering journal to track your progress and reflect on the benefits of an organized space:

- Note the areas of your home that feel most cluttered and why.
- Reflect on which items truly bring you joy and which you can let go.
- Document your experiences with decluttering, noting how it impacts your mood and productivity.
- Set goals for maintaining an organized space and celebrate your successes along the way.

This exercise not only aids in the physical process of decluttering but also nurtures a mindful approach to living, emphasizing the value of simplicity and intentionality in creating a peaceful home.

## 8.5 UNDERSTANDING RENT AGREEMENTS AND HOUSING OPTIONS

Navigating the world of rent agreements can seem daunting, but understanding the basics makes it much easier. When you look at a lease agreement, pay close attention to the rent amount and due date. These figures dictate your monthly financial commitment, so ensure they align with your budget. The terms for a security deposit and lease duration are also crucial. The deposit typically acts as a safeguard against damages, and knowing the lease length helps you plan your stay. Some agreements might be month-to-month, while others require a year-long commitment. Understanding these components helps you avoid surprises and prepares you for a smooth rental experience.

Exploring different housing options is an exciting part of independent living. Apartments and shared housing offer varied experiences. Apartments provide privacy and personal space, ideal for those who value independence. On the other hand, shared housing, like a room in a house, can be more cost-effective and often fosters a sense of community. Renting a studio versus a one-bedroom apartment involves weighing the pros and cons. Studios are typically more affordable and easier to maintain, perfect for minimalists or those on a budget. One-bedroom apartments offer additional space, making them suitable for those needing a separate living area. Consider your lifestyle and needs when choosing the right option.

Knowing your rights and responsibilities as a tenant empowers you to maintain a harmonious living situation. You have the right to request timely repairs, making sure your living space is safe and functional. Whether it's a leaky roof or a malfunctioning heater, landlords are usually obliged to address such issues promptly. Maintaining property cleanliness and safety is your responsibility, ensuring a pleasant living environment for you and your neighbors. Understanding these rights and responsibilities fosters a respectful relationship between tenants and landlords, preventing misunderstandings and promoting a healthy living space.

The rental application process can seem like a maze, but breaking it down makes it manageable. Start by gathering necessary documents like pay stubs proving your ability to meet rent obligations. A rental resume outlining your rental history, references, and employment details can set you apart from other applicants. It provides landlords with a snapshot of your reliability as a tenant. Be honest and thorough, as transparency builds trust. Once you have your documentation ready, you can schedule viewings to explore potential homes. During these visits, ask questions about the property and lease terms to ensure they suit your needs. After selecting a place, submit your application promptly. This proactive approach shows that you are interested and ready to move forward.

***Interactive Element: Rental Application Checklist***

Create a checklist to streamline your rental application journey:

- List the documents needed: pay stubs, ID, rental history, and references.
- Prepare a rental resume: highlight your reliability and employment details.
- Schedule viewings: ask questions about the lease and property.
- Submit applications: be prompt and thorough to showcase interest.

This checklist keeps you organized and focused, guiding you through each step of securing a new home.

## 8.6 MANAGING UTILITY BILLS AND SUBSCRIPTIONS

Understanding how to read and interpret utility bills is fundamental in managing household expenses. Each month, these bills arrive, detailing the costs of electricity, water, and gas usage. Electricity bills often break down charges based on kilowatt-hours (kWh) used. Pay attention to peak usage charges, which apply when energy demand is highest, typically in the afternoon and early evening. You can adjust your usage by identifying these peak times, perhaps running major appliances during off-peak hours to save money. Water bills reflect gallons or cubic meters consumption, with charges based on usage levels. Conserving water by taking shorter showers or fixing leaks can significantly reduce these costs. Gas bills, similar to electricity, may include a base charge plus usage. Understanding each component helps you pinpoint where you can cut back, making these bills less daunting and more manageable.

Reducing utility costs saves money and promotes energy efficiency, benefiting your wallet and the environment. Simple actions like turning off lights when leaving a room can accumulate savings over time. Consider investing in energy-efficient LED bulbs, which use less electricity and last longer than traditional bulbs. Sealing drafts around windows and doors is another effective strategy. A small tube of caulk or weather stripping can prevent heat loss in the winter and keep your home cooler in the summer. This not only lowers heating and cooling expenses but also enhances comfort. Additionally, unplugging devices when not in use and using power strips can prevent "phantom" energy loss, further reducing costs. When practiced consistently, these small changes contribute to a noticeable decrease in utility expenses, fostering a more sustainable lifestyle.

Managing monthly subscriptions has become an integral part of budgeting in today's digital age. From streaming services to gym memberships, these recurring charges can quickly add up. To keep track, consider using apps designed to monitor subscriptions. These tools provide an overview of all active services, alerting you to upcoming payments and helping you identify any subscriptions you no longer need. Regularly reviewing this list can prevent unnecessary expenses and free up funds for other priorities. It's also wise to evaluate whether you're getting value from each service; canceling or downgrading can save money. This proactive approach ensures that your subscriptions align with your lifestyle and budget, avoiding the trap of paying for forgotten or underused services.

Setting up automatic payments for utility bills and subscriptions simplifies financial management, ensuring you never miss a due date. Late fees can accumulate quickly, impacting your budget and credit score. By automating payments, you guarantee timely transactions, reducing stress and eliminating the risk of oversight. Start by deciding which bills to automate—essential ones like utilities and rent should be prioritized. Once set up through your bank or service provider, you can enjoy peace of mind, knowing your obligations are met without constant monitoring. This system streamlines your financial routine and allows you to focus on other aspects of independent living, reinforcing responsible money management habits.

As you master these independent living skills, remember that each step builds a foundation for future success. Understanding and managing utility bills and subscriptions are key components of a stable and organized life. These strategies empower you to take control of your expenses, promoting financial independence and sustainability. With these skills, you're well-equipped to face the challenges of adulthood, paving the way for a balanced and fulfilling life. Now, with this knowledge, you can confidently approach the next chapter, ready to tackle new dimensions of personal growth and self-sufficiency.

# 9

# COMMUNITY ENGAGEMENT AND SOCIAL RESPONSIBILITY

*"We rise by lifting others."*

— ROBERT INGERSOLL

Imagine walking into a community center bustling with activity. A group of teens is organizing a food drive, another is preparing for a neighborhood cleanup, and a few others are planning an educational workshop for local kids. The energy is contagious, and you can't help but feel drawn into the collective spirit of giving back. This vibrant scene is more than just a gathering of people; it's a testament to the power of community engagement and the profound impact volunteering has on individuals and the broader community. It's a place where every effort, big or small, contributes to a tapestry of positive change.

## 9.1 THE IMPORTANCE OF VOLUNTEERING AND COMMUNITY SERVICE

Volunteering offers numerous benefits that extend beyond meeting community service requirements. It is a journey of personal growth, fostering empathy, compassion, and a deeper understanding of the world around you. When you volunteer, you step into someone else's shoes, experiencing their struggles and triumphs alongside them. This builds empathy, allowing you to connect with others on a human level. It's a powerful feeling—knowing that your actions, no matter how small, can make a significant difference in someone's life. This sense of contribution enriches your life with purpose and fulfillment.

Moreover, volunteering helps develop essential leadership and teamwork skills. Working alongside diverse groups of people teaches you how to communicate effectively, resolve conflicts, and collaborate toward a common goal. These skills are invaluable, not just in community service but in every aspect of life. They prepare you for challenges, enabling you to lead with confidence and work harmoniously in teams. As you take on responsibilities and lead initiatives, you cultivate a sense of ownership and accountability, qualities that are highly sought after in both academic and professional settings.

Finding the right volunteer opportunity can feel overwhelming, especially with so many causes and organizations seeking support. However, aligning your interests with your volunteer work can transform the experience from a duty to a passion. Platforms like VolunteerMatch make this process easier by connecting you with opportunities that align with your interests and schedule. Whether you're passionate about environmental conservation, education, or healthcare, there's a place for you to contribute. Local community centers and nonprofits are also excellent resources; they often welcome volunteers with open arms, eager to benefit from your unique talents and perspectives.

Volunteering is not just about giving back; it's also a gateway to exploring potential career paths. For aspiring medical professionals, volunteering in healthcare settings provides invaluable insights into the industry. You gain firsthand experience, observing professionals in action and understanding the challenges they face. Similarly, participating in environmental projects offers a glimpse into the world of sustainability, exposing you to the intricacies of conservation work. These experiences enrich your understanding and help you make informed decisions about your future career. They offer a practical perspective, allowing you to assess whether a particular field aligns with your interests and values.

Creating a volunteering plan can maximize the impact of your efforts. You can start by setting clear goals, such as a target number of volunteer hours each month. This keeps you committed and allows you to track your progress and see the tangible results of your contributions. Reflect on the impact of your work and how it aligns with your personal growth. Are there new skills you've developed? Have you made meaningful connections? Documenting these experiences can be incredibly rewarding, providing a sense of achievement and motivation to continue your efforts. A structured plan ensures that your volunteer work is not just a one-time event but a sustained commitment to making a difference.

*Reflection Section: Volunteering Journal*

Consider keeping a volunteering journal to capture your experiences and insights. Reflect on the following prompts:

- What volunteer activities have you participated in recently?
- How have these experiences impacted your understanding of the community and yourself?
- What new skills or insights have you gained through volunteering?
- How do you plan to continue your volunteer efforts in the future?

Use this journal to track your growth and celebrate the positive impact you're making in your community. Through volunteering, you contribute to the betterment of society and embark on a journey of self-discovery and personal development.

## 9.2 UNDERSTANDING SOCIAL CAUSES AND ADVOCACY

In the hustle and bustle of everyday life, it's easy to overlook the pressing issues that impact our communities and the world. Yet, understanding these social issues is the first step toward meaningful change. Take a moment to think about the problems that catch your attention—perhaps it's the sight of homelessness on your way to school or news reports about education inequality. These are not just distant statistics; they are real challenges affecting real people and call for our awareness and action. Researching these issues locally and globally can open your eyes to the complexities of poverty, access to education, and countless other concerns. By staying informed, you position yourself to contribute to solutions. Explore reliable sources and data to gain a deeper understanding of the challenges we face, which can spark the passion needed to drive change.

Advocacy plays a pivotal role in addressing these social issues, offering a powerful avenue for teens to influence change. It's about raising your voice and using it to make a difference, whether through writing letters to elected officials or participating in peaceful protests. When you write to those in power, you bring attention to causes that matter, urging them to take action. A well-crafted letter can highlight the urgency of an issue and propose tangible solutions. Meanwhile, joining peaceful protests or campaigns allows you to stand alongside others who share your commitment, amplifying your message and drawing public attention to the cause. Advocacy isn't just about speaking up; it's about creating a ripple effect, inspiring others to join the movement and work toward a common goal. Through these efforts, you contribute to social change, helping to shape a more equitable and just society.

Social media has revolutionized the way we engage with advocacy, offering a platform to raise awareness and mobilize support like never before. With just a few clicks, you can create informative posts that spread the word about important causes, reaching an audience far beyond your immediate circle. Infographics, videos, and personal stories can capture attention and encourage others to learn more. Collaborating with online advocacy groups can further expand your reach, connecting you with like-minded individuals and organizations. Together, you can coordinate efforts, share resources, and launch campaigns that draw attention to the issues at hand. Social media transforms advocacy from a solitary effort into a community-driven movement, where voices unite to demand change. It's a tool that, when used thoughtfully, has the potential to engage and empower, turning awareness into action.

Developing an advocacy plan is crucial for focusing your efforts and maximizing your impact. Start by setting clear objectives for your advocacy work. What do you hope to achieve, and how will you measure success? These goals will guide your activities and ensure that your efforts remain purposeful and effective. Next, create a timeline for your advocacy efforts, outlining specific actions and deadlines. Breaking down the process into manageable steps helps maintain momentum and track progress. Consider the resources you'll need, from informational materials to support from peers and mentors. As you develop your plan, stay flexible and open to feedback, adapting your approach as necessary to overcome challenges. This strategic planning strengthens your advocacy work and builds skills in organization and leadership.

***Interactive Element: Advocacy Plan Template***

To help you get started, consider using this Advocacy Plan Template:

- **Objective:** Define the specific change you aim to achieve.
- **Research:** Identify key facts and statistics that support your cause.
- **Target Audience:** Determine who needs to hear your message (e.g., local officials, community members).
- **Key Messages:** Craft clear, compelling messages that convey the importance of your cause.
- **Action Steps:** Outline specific actions you'll take, such as organizing events or creating content.
- **Timeline:** Set deadlines for each action to maintain focus and accountability.
- **Evaluation:** Plan how you'll assess the effectiveness of your advocacy efforts.

An organized approach can enhance your efforts, making your advocacy more impactful and rewarding.

## 9.3 PRACTICING ENVIRONMENTAL SUSTAINABILITY

Consider the impact of your daily actions on the environment. Each choice you make, from the products you buy to the energy you consume, contributes to your carbon footprint. This is the total amount of greenhouse gases emitted directly or indirectly by your activities. Calculating your carbon footprint can be an eye-opener, revealing how everyday habits add up. For instance, driving a car, using electricity, and even the food you eat all contribute to this tally. Understanding this helps you identify areas where you can reduce your impact. Similarly, think about the plastic waste that ends up in our oceans, harming marine life and ecosystems. Plastic bottles, bags, and microplastics pose a significant threat to sea creatures, often mistaking them for food. Recognizing these impacts emphasizes the need for change, urging you to adopt more sustainable practices.

Incorporating sustainability into your daily life doesn't have to be overwhelming. Start with small, practical changes that make a difference. Reducing single-use plastics is a great place to begin. Opt for reusable water bottles and shopping bags instead of disposable ones. This simple switch can significantly cut down on waste. At home, implement energy-saving habits. Turn off lights when leaving a room and unplug devices when not in use. These actions not only conserve energy but also lower utility bills. Additionally, consider using energy-efficient appliances, which consume less power and are better for the environment. When practiced consistently, these small steps create a ripple effect, contributing to a healthier planet.

Getting involved in environmental initiatives amplifies your impact. Local clean-up events are a fantastic way to contribute to environmental health while connecting with like-minded individuals. These events often focus on removing litter from beaches, parks, and neighborhoods, preventing pollution from reaching waterways. Participating provides a tangible sense of achievement as you see the immediate results of your efforts. Tree-planting campaigns are another impactful activity. Trees absorb carbon dioxide, improve air quality, and provide habitats for wildlife. By supporting these campaigns, you actively contribute to combating climate change and fostering biodiversity. These initiatives enhance the environment and instill a sense of community and shared purpose.

Inspiring others to embrace sustainable practices can multiply your efforts. Lead by example in your school or community, perhaps by initiating a recycling program. Educate peers about the importance of recycling and how it reduces waste in landfills. Organize workshops or presentations that highlight the benefits of sustainability, encouraging others to adopt eco-friendly habits. Share tips and resources, making it easy for people to incorporate changes into their routines. Encouragement and education can spark interest and motivation, creating a culture of sustainability. By fostering awareness and action, you empower those around you to make environmentally conscious decisions, amplifying the positive impact on the planet.

## 9.4 ENGAGING IN CIVIC DUTIES AND RESPONSIBILITIES

Imagine being part of a community where your voice matters and where your actions contribute to the greater good. This is what civic responsibility is all about. It's the idea that each of us has a role to play in shaping the communities we live in. Participating in community meetings is a great way to start. These gatherings offer a platform to discuss local issues, propose solutions, and collaborate with others who share your passion for change.

Understanding how local government structures work can also demystify the processes that affect your daily life. It equips you with the knowledge to advocate for improvements and hold officials accountable. Civic engagement is about being informed and active, ensuring that your community reflects the values and needs of its members. By participating, you strengthen the social fabric, fostering a sense of unity and shared purpose.

Voting is a cornerstone of civic duty, a powerful tool that allows individuals to influence policies and elect leaders who align with their values. For teens approaching voting age, understanding the process is crucial. Registering to vote is the first step. It's a simple yet significant action that opens the door to participation in local, state, and national elections. Take the time to learn about the candidates and issues on the ballot. This knowledge empowers you to make informed decisions that resonate with your beliefs and priorities. Engage in discussions with peers and family, sharing insights and perspectives. This exchange of ideas enriches your understanding and prepares you for future participation. Voting is not just a right; it's a responsibility that shapes the direction of your community and country.

But civic engagement extends beyond the ballot box. There are numerous ways to contribute to the democratic process and ensure your voice is heard. Volunteering for political campaigns is one such avenue. It offers a behind-the-scenes look at how campaigns operate and provides a platform to support candidates who champion causes you care about. Whether it's phone banking, canvassing, or organizing events, each task contributes to the momentum of the campaign. Attending town halls and public forums is another impactful way to engage. These events offer direct access to elected officials, allowing you to ask questions and express concerns. They foster transparency and accountability, ensuring that representatives remain attuned to the needs of their constituents. Civic involvement is about creating a dialogue between the public and those in power, ensuring that governance reflects the will of the people.

Fostering a culture of civic engagement among peers can amplify the impact of your efforts. Consider organizing a civic engagement club at school. This initiative can serve as a hub for students interested in discussing current events, learning about political processes, and planning community projects. Creating a dialogue and action space encourages others to explore their civic identities and contribute to meaningful change. The club can host guest speakers, organize voter registration drives, and participate in community service projects. These activities not only educate but also inspire a sense of agency and responsibility. You lay the groundwork for a more informed and active society by nurturing a community of engaged citizens.

Civic duties are the pillars upon which strong communities are built. They call on each of us to engage, participate, and work towards collective well-being. As we carry these principles forward, they guide us in fostering societies that are both inclusive and responsive to the needs of all.

# 10

# PLANNING FOR THE FUTURE

*"You are never too young to start an empire and never too old to chase a new dream."*

— ANONYMOUS

Picture yourself at the edge of a bustling high school hallway at the end of your final year. The bell rings, signaling the close of one chapter and the imminent start of another. As you step into the next phase of life, questions about what lies ahead swirl in your mind. The transition from school to work is a pivotal moment filled with both excitement and uncertainty. Navigating this path requires more than just academic knowledge; it demands practical skills and strategies to bridge the gap between education and career. This chapter equips you with the tools to chart your course, emphasizing the importance of networking, gaining experience, developing transferable skills, and balancing work with personal life.

## 10.1 NAVIGATING THE TRANSITION FROM SCHOOL TO WORK

Building a professional network is a crucial step toward creating opportunities in your desired industry. Networking is not just about collecting contacts; it's about forming meaningful relationships that can lead to growth and collaboration. Start by utilizing platforms like LinkedIn, a powerful tool for connecting with industry professionals and staying updated on industry trends. Think of LinkedIn as your digital business card—keep your profile polished and professional, highlighting your skills and achievements. Engage with content relevant to your field, join groups, and participate in discussions to increase your visibility. In addition to online networking, attending industry-related conferences and events offers a chance to meet influential people face-to-face. These gatherings are fertile grounds for networking, where you can exchange ideas, learn from experts, and possibly find mentors. Remember, each interaction is an opportunity to expand your network and open doors to future possibilities.

Gaining relevant experience is another vital aspect of transitioning from school to work. Internships, part-time jobs, and volunteering provide hands-on experience that enhances your resume and builds your skill set. When applying for internships, focus on those that align with your career interests. This gives you a taste of your chosen field and helps you determine if it's the right fit for you. Additionally, seek mentorship opportunities within organizations. Mentors can offer guidance, share insights from their experiences, and help you navigate challenges. Volunteering, though often overlooked, is also a valuable way to gain experience and give back to the community. It demonstrates initiative and commitment, qualities that employers appreciate. Each of these experiences contributes to your growth, preparing you for the demands of the workforce.

Developing transferable skills is essential, as these abilities are valuable across various job roles and industries. Skills like effective communication and teamwork are universal and crucial in any workplace. Communication involves more than just speaking—it's about listening, writing clearly, and presenting ideas confidently. Teamwork, on the other hand, requires collaboration, patience, and the ability to work harmoniously with others. Problem-solving and adaptability are equally important. The modern workplace is dynamic, and the ability to think critically and adapt to change is highly prized. These skills make you a more attractive candidate and prepare you to handle the diverse challenges you may face in your career. Cultivate these abilities through practice and by seeking feedback, ensuring you're ready to excel in any environment.

Creating a work-life balance plan is the final piece of the puzzle. As you transition from school to work, it's vital to establish a balance between your professional responsibilities and personal life. Start by setting boundaries for work hours. Decide when you'll focus on work and when you'll disconnect to recharge. This separation helps prevent burnout and ensures that work doesn't encroach on your personal time. Prioritizing self-care and leisure activities is equally important. Allocate time for hobbies, exercise, and relaxation to maintain your mental and physical well-being. Remember, a balanced life leads to greater productivity and satisfaction, both at work and in your personal life. Finding this balance is an ongoing process, requiring adjustments as your responsibilities and priorities evolve.

***Interactive Element: Networking Reflection Exercise***

Take a moment to reflect on your current network. Consider the following questions and jot down your thoughts:

- Who are the key people in your existing network, and how can you strengthen these relationships?
- What steps can you take to expand your network? Think about attending events, joining online forums, or reaching out to industry professionals.
- How can you provide value to your network? Consider ways you can offer support, share knowledge, or connect others.

This exercise helps you assess your networking efforts and identify areas for growth, ensuring you build a strong, supportive network that benefits your career.

As you navigate the transition from school to work, these strategies will guide you toward a successful and fulfilling career. Embrace the opportunities to learn and grow, knowing that each step you take lays the foundation for your future.

## 10.2 FINANCIAL PLANNING FOR FUTURE STABILITY

Imagine a day when you no longer have to worry about unexpected expenses or financial emergencies. Achieving this level of peace of mind begins with understanding the basics of investing. Investing is a powerful tool to grow your wealth over time, and it starts with familiarizing yourself with the fundamental concepts of stocks, bonds, and mutual funds. Stocks represent ownership in a company, allowing you to share in its profits and growth. On the other hand, bonds are a form of lending money to a corporation or government in exchange for periodic interest payments. Mutual funds pool money from many investors to purchase a diversified portfolio of stocks and bonds. Each of these investment vehicles offers different levels of risk and potential return, making it important to consider your financial goals and risk tolerance before diving in. One of the most exciting aspects of investing is the power of compound interest. By reinvesting your earnings, you can earn interest on both your initial investment and the accumulated interest over time. This snowball effect can significantly boost your wealth, especially when you start investing early.

As mentioned previously, establishing a savings and emergency fund is another crucial step in your financial journey. A well-thought-out savings plan acts as a safety net, providing financial security in times of need. Begin by setting a specific savings goal for emergencies. This fund should ideally cover three to six months of living expenses, ensuring you can handle unexpected situations like job loss or medical emergencies without financial stress. To make saving easier, consider automating your savings contributions. By setting up automatic transfers from your checking account to your savings account, you can build your fund consistently without having to think about it. This approach helps you stay disciplined and allows your savings to grow steadily over time. Remember, the key to successful saving is consistency, no matter how small the amount. Over time, these contributions add up, providing peace of mind and financial stability.

Managing debt responsibly is an integral part of financial planning. Whether it's student loans or credit card debt, having a strategy in place can help you reduce and eventually eliminate debt. Start by creating a plan to pay off high-interest debt first. This approach, known as the avalanche method, focuses on reducing the most expensive debt, saving you money on interest payments in the long run. Another strategy is the snowball method, where you pay off smaller debts first to build momentum and confidence as you see quick progress. Both methods have their benefits, so choose the one that best suits your financial situation and preferences. Additionally, avoid accumulating new debt whenever possible. Create a realistic budget that accounts for debt payments, and stick to it. By managing your debt effectively, you free up resources to invest in your future, paving the way for financial freedom.

Planning for retirement may seem like a distant concern, but starting early can make a significant difference in your financial future. Opening a Roth IRA is a great starting point. This type of retirement account allows your contributions to grow tax-free, and you won't be taxed on withdrawals in retirement, provided certain conditions are met. It's an excellent option for young investors who expect to be in a higher tax bracket in the future. Understanding employer-sponsored retirement plans, such as 401(k)s, is also essential. Many employers offer matching contributions, which are essentially free money, so take advantage of this benefit by contributing enough to receive the full match. Even if retirement feels far off, small contributions made consistently over time can lead to substantial savings. The earlier you start, the more time you allow your investments to grow, thanks to the power of compound interest. It's about building a solid financial foundation now to enjoy a secure and prosperous retirement later.

In the ever-evolving landscape of personal finance, staying informed and proactive is key. This involves understanding the basics of investing, saving, and managing debt, continuously seeking knowledge, and adapting to new financial tools and strategies. As you progress through life, your financial goals and circumstances will change, requiring you to reassess and adjust your plans. By keeping an open mind and remaining flexible, you can navigate the complexities of financial planning with confidence. Remember, the choices you make today have a lasting impact on your financial well-being, so take the time to educate yourself and make informed decisions.

## 10.3 LONG-TERM GOAL SETTING AND LIFE PLANNING

Imagine standing at the helm of your life, steering towards the horizon. It's a powerful image that encapsulates the essence of long-term goal-setting and life planning. The first step in this process is to create a vision for your future. This means taking the time to reflect on what you truly want out of life—not just in terms of a career, but also personal happiness and fulfillment. Start by writing a personal mission statement. This statement acts as a compass, guiding your decisions and actions. It should encapsulate your core values and aspirations, acting as a reminder of what you're working towards when the path becomes challenging. Visualizing your life in 10, 20, and 30 years can also be a helpful exercise. Picture where you want to live, what kind of work you want to do, and how you want to spend your time. This visualization helps clarify your long-term goals, providing a clearer roadmap for your journey through life.

Once you have a vision, the next step is to develop an action plan for your life goals. This involves breaking down your long-term aspirations into manageable steps. Consider what milestones you need to reach for each major goal. For example, if you dream of becoming a doctor, your milestones include completing a pre-med program, passing the MCAT, and applying to medical school. Identifying the resources and support you need is also crucial.

This might involve finding mentors, seeking educational opportunities, or gaining relevant experience. An action plan serves as a blueprint, detailing the steps you need to take and the support you'll require along the way. It transforms abstract dreams into concrete actions, making them more attainable and less daunting.

Life, as we all know, is unpredictable. Circumstances change, and plans must adapt to remain relevant. This is why flexibility is an integral part of life planning. Regularly revisiting your goals ensures they align with your evolving circumstances and priorities. Consider setting aside time each year to review your progress and make necessary adjustments. Ask yourself if your goals still resonate with you or if they need refinement. Maybe you've discovered a new passion, or perhaps life events have shifted your priorities. Whatever the case, being open to change is essential. Flexibility doesn't mean abandoning your goals; it means navigating life's twists and turns with grace and resilience.

As you plan for the future, it's important not to lose sight of the balance between personal and professional aspirations. While career success is critical, so is personal fulfillment. Consider how your hobbies and passions can be integrated into your life plans. Maybe you love painting or playing music—find ways to incorporate these activities into your routine, even if they don't directly relate to your career. Pursuing passions enriches your personal life and can fuel creativity and innovation in your professional endeavors. Striking this balance ensures a well-rounded life where work and personal interests coexist harmoniously. It's about creating a life that reflects all facets of who you are, not just your professional identity.

In the grand tapestry of life, goal setting and planning are the threads that weave together your ambitions, dreams, and realities. By creating a vision, developing an action plan, adapting to change, and balancing aspirations, you lay the groundwork for a future filled with purpose and fulfillment. Remember, the journey of life is as much about the experiences along the way as it is about reaching the destination. As you move forward, embrace each step with curiosity and determination, knowing that you are crafting your own future.

# THANK YOU

Thank you for investing your time in **Life Skills for Teens**. I hope you enjoyed reading the book as much as I enjoyed writing it.

If you found it helpful, please take just a minute or two to share your thoughts with other teens, young adults and parents by writing a quick review to let them know how it might help them, too.

Simply scan the QR code:

Thanks again.

Wishing you great success and a prosperous future!

AC Bradford

# CONCLUSION

As you reach the end of this guide, it's time to reflect on the journey we've taken together. Throughout the chapters, we've delved into various life skills crucial for transitioning into adulthood. From mastering social skills and understanding financial literacy to managing technology, navigating healthcare, and embracing independent living, each aspect plays a vital role in preparing you for a successful future. These skills are not just about surviving but thriving in an ever-evolving world.

The lessons we've covered are stepping stones toward becoming confident in handling real-world responsibilities. Financial independence is more than just managing money; it's about making informed decisions that secure your future. Maintaining personal well-being ensures that you can face life's challenges with resilience and grace. Engaging with your community and social causes fosters a sense of belonging and purpose, reminding us of the power of collective action.

I hope this book has transformed your perspective, moving you from feeling overwhelmed to feeling capable and self-assured. The journey of personal growth is ongoing, and the skills you've learned are tools to navigate it. As you continue to grow, remember that each skill you develop is a step toward empowerment and independence.

Learning doesn't stop here. I encourage you to seek out additional resources and opportunities to further enhance your skills. Consider attending workshops, enrolling in online courses, or participating in community events. Each of these experiences will deepen your understanding and provide practical applications of what you've learned. The more you explore, the more adept you become at tackling life's diverse challenges.

My passion for helping teens like you navigate adulthood stems from my own experiences and challenges. I know firsthand how daunting the transition can be. When I was your age, I faced similar uncertainties and questions. This personal journey fuels my commitment to empower you with the knowledge and tools needed to succeed. I believe in your potential and am honored to be part of your journey.

As you step forward, I urge you to apply the skills and strategies we've discussed in your daily life. Share your newfound knowledge with friends and peers. Lead by example and inspire others to embark on personal growth paths. Take proactive steps in your personal and professional development, knowing that you have the foundation to build a fulfilling and successful life.

Thank you for investing in your personal growth and for joining me on this journey. Your courage to take the first steps toward mastering life skills is commendable. I appreciate your trust and commitment to becoming the best version of yourself.

Remember, mastering life skills is not just about achieving independence and confidence; it's about embracing a journey of lifelong learning and personal development. Each step you take brings you closer to the adult you aspire to be. Embrace this journey with enthusiasm and curiosity; it is the path to a fulfilling and successful future.

# REFERENCES

*The 8 best budgeting & money apps for kids & teens* https://www.gohenry.com/uk/blog/financial-education/the-best-budgeting-apps-for-families

*Financial Education & Resources for Students & Young ...* https://promotions.bankofamerica.com/student-banking

*Why Is It Important to Establish Credit When Young?* https://www.experian.com/blogs/ask-experian/why-it-is-important-to-establish-credit-when-you-are-young/

*10 Common Scams Targeted at Teens* https://www.investopedia.com/financial-edge/1012/common-scams-targeted-at-teens.aspx

*The 13 Essential Traits of Good Friends* https://www.psychologytoday.com/us/blog/lifetime-connections/201503/the-13-essential-traits-good-friends

*5 Conflict Resolution Strategies* https://www.pon.harvard.edu/daily/conflict-resolution/conflict-resolution-strategies/

*Setting Healthy Boundaries in Relationships* https://www.helpguide.org/relationships/social-connection/setting-healthy-boundaries-in-relationships

*Beyond the Sex Talks: Teaching Teens Emotional Intimacy* https://educateempowerkids.org/emotional-intimacy/

*Self-Esteem vs. Self-Confidence: What's the Difference?* https://mentalhealthcenterkids.com/blogs/articles/self-esteem-vs-self-confidence

*Cognitive Empathy vs. Emotional Empathy* https://www.verywellmind.com/cognitive-and-emotional-empathy-4582389

*J.K. Rowling on How to Deal With Failure in Life and Work* https://mayooshin.com/j-k-rowling-how-to-deal-with-failure-in-life

*15 Strategies For Cultivating A Growth Mindset In Teens & ...* https://lifeskillsadvocate.com/blog/15-strategies-to-help-teens-adults-overcome-a-fixed-mindset/

*First impressions count* https://www.apa.org/gradpsych/2012/11/first-impressions

*5 Ways to Be an Active Listener for Your Teen* https://www.newportacademy.com/resources/empowering-teens/active-listener/

*How to Apologize Sincerely and Effectively: 9 Tips* https://www.verywellmind.com/how-to-apologize-more-sincerely-3144467

*Social Anxiety (for Teens)* https://kidshealth.org/en/teens/social-phobia.html

*Importance of Good Personal Hygiene for Teenagers - Lesson* https://study.com/academy/lesson/importance-of-good-personal-hygiene-for-teenagers.html#:

# 132 | REFERENCES

*How to prepare your teen to manage their own medical care* https://health.choc.org/how-to-prepare-your-teen-to-manage-their-own-medical-care/

*Stress Management and Teens* https://www.aacap.org/AACAP/Families_and_Youth/Facts_for_Families/FFF-Guide/Helping-Teenagers-With-Stress-066.aspx

*Teen Mental Health: How to Know When Your Child Needs ...* https://www.healthychildren.org/English/ages-stages/teen/Pages/Mental-Health-and-Teens-Watch-for-Danger-Signs.aspx

*Digital Etiquette for Teenagers* https://medium.com/@phyllisguwe/digital-etiquette-for-teenagers-613c2040f9f1

*Effects of Excessive Screen Time on Child Development* https://www.ncbi.nlm.nih.gov/pmc/articles/PMC10353947/

*Creating Strong Passwords and Other Ways To Protect ...* https://consumer.ftc.gov/articles/creating-strong-passwords-and-other-ways-protect-your-accounts

*Teachers' Essential Guide to Cyberbullying Prevention* https://www.commonsense.org/education/articles/teachers-essential-guide-to-cyberbullying-prevention

*SMART Goals for Students* https://www.purdueglobal.edu/blog/student-life/smart-goals-for-students/

*7 Effective Study Techniques for High School Students* https://studyworkgrow.com/7-effective-study-techniques-for-high-school-students/

*Federal Student Aid (FAFSA)* https://studentaid.gov/h/apply-for-aid/fafsa

*How to Write a Great Resume and Cover Letter* https://extension.harvard.edu/blog/how-to-write-a-great-resume-and-cover-letter/

*5 Home Maintenance Skills Every Teen Should Learn* https://skilltrekker.com/5-home-maintenance-skills-for-teens/

*Meal Planning 101: A Complete Beginner's Guide to ...* https://www.everydayhealth.com/diet-nutrition/meal-planning/

*12 Cooking Skills Every Young Adult Should Learn - Cookist* https://www.cookist.com/12-cooking-skills-every-young-adult-should-learn/

*Understanding Leases and Rental Agreements & Their ...* https://www.justia.com/real-estate/landlord-tenant/information-for-tenants/understanding-your-lease-or-rental-agreement/

*The Benefits of Teen Volunteerism: Transforming Lives and ...* https://www.nvfs.org/benefits-of-teen-volunteerism/

*VolunteerMatch - Where Volunteering Begins* https://www.volunteermatch.org/

*Social Media Has Changed the Advocacy Landscape Forever* https://www.naylor.com/associationadviser/social-media-has-changed-the-advocacy-landscape-forever/#:

*Sustainable Living for Young Adults: How to Embrace ...* https://www.elephantjournal.

com/2024/03/sustainable-living-for-young-adults-how-to-embrace-environ mental-consciousness-in-your-20s-madeline-lillis/

*The Value of Networking As a Teen: 10 Ways to make ...* https://futurenorth.ca/the-value-of-networking-as-a-teen-10-ways-to-make-meaningful-connections-with-the-right-people/

*7 Ways for Students to Gain Work Experience* http://www.letsgettoworkwi.org/wp-content/uploads/2014/09/7-Ways-to-Gain-Work-Exp-web-FINAL-9-8-14.pdf

*The Young Person's Guide to Investing* https://www.nytimes.com/2020/02/10/smarter-living/the-young-persons-guide-to-investing.html

*Charting the Future: A Teen's Guide to Effective Life Planning* https://theattitudeadvantage.com/all-posts/charting-the-future-a-teens-guide-to-effective-life-planning/

Made in United States
Orlando, FL
10 January 2025